Praise for

FRANCIS TOP'S GRAND DESIGN

"In the liminal space between reality and dream, Craig Rodgers' sly and subtle stories track the lives of artists, misfits, and drifters. This huge-hearted collection will welcome you in and knock you out."

—Ryan Ridge, author of *New Bad News* and *Ox*

"Inhabited by oddball characters resigned to the knowledge the universe is laughing at them, the stories in *Francis Top's Grand Design* teem with the kind of deadpan surrealism found in Lynch and Brautigan. Craig Rodgers calmly guides the reader to the edge of the abyss, but he never tells them to look inside because he knows we're going to do that anyway."

—Jeff Chon, author of *Hashtag Good Guy With a Gun*

Craig Rodgers' work puts an eye to the cracks of reality, seeing strange movement in its darkness. A collection vibrating with uneasy mysteries that don't leave you. You won't regret reading this.

—Tiffany Belieu

Francis Top's Grand Design recalls masters of existential horror such as Franz Kafka and Brian Evenson. These sharp, stark tales run on estrangement, obsession, and the unsolved mysteries at the shriveled heart of contemporary life.

—Jennifer Wortman, author of *This. This. This. Is. Love. Love. Love.*

"There's this magical moment in a very special kind of movie-watching experience. Where you, the viewer, maybe in a darkened theater, maybe at home fully engrossed, having completely lost track of time, think to yourself: "it should end right here," characters mid-thought and the film fully understanding its own weight. And then it does. It cuts to credits and you feel the warmth of art executed exactly to your needs. Craig Rodgers' stories exist in that perfect moment. *Francis Top's Grand Design* is full of miniature movies that you never want to end, but of course they have to, and we're all the better for it when they do."

—KKUURRTT, author of *Good at Drugs*

Francis Top's Grand Design

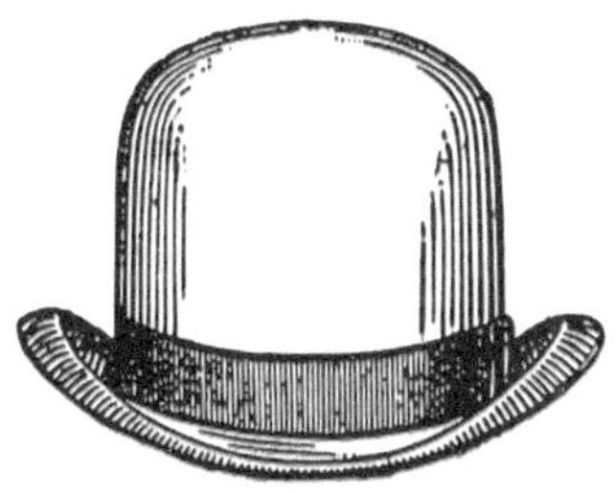

Craig Rodgers

DEATH OF PRINT

Francis Top's Grand Design is a work of fiction. It's all made up. Published by Death of Print. Typesetting by Alan Good. Cover design by Tiffany Belieu.

Print ISBN: 9781088024645
Ebook ISBN: 9781088024676

Deathofprint.press

Some of the stories are previously published:

-The Weather Maker
- Back Patio Press - 2 June 2019
- Drowning
- Faded Out - 2018? - DEFUNCT
- The Rails
- Apocalypse Confidential - 8 Mar 2022
- A Man with Goals
- Train Magazine - 2018? - no longer online
- Man in Leaf
- Juked - Nov 2014
- Doing Time
- Twist in Time Magazine Issues 5 and 6 - serialized
- 1 Sept 2019 and 1 Nov 2019

Also by Craig Rodgers

DEATH OF PRINT

The Ghost of Mile 43

One More Number

TWISTIT PRESS

Moonbeams

Twenty Ponds

A NOTE

What is this book? It's a set of stories, one after the other. It's a collection, but it isn't any one thing. It's not horror, but if some night down the road you wake from a nightmare of something met herein, I would understand. It's not mystery, but there are questions that will go unanswered. Is it literary? Pal, I don't even know what that means.

One of these stories came out of an offhand comment about a poolboy. Another was first envisioned as a painting. Not the one you'll find yourself thinking. One was a dream.

My friend and editor Alan Good says everything I write is a ghost story. The oldest of these stories was written in April 2007. The newest is still being written.

Craig Rodgers
1/15/2022

Alan, Cavin, Nadia, Renee,

Thank you

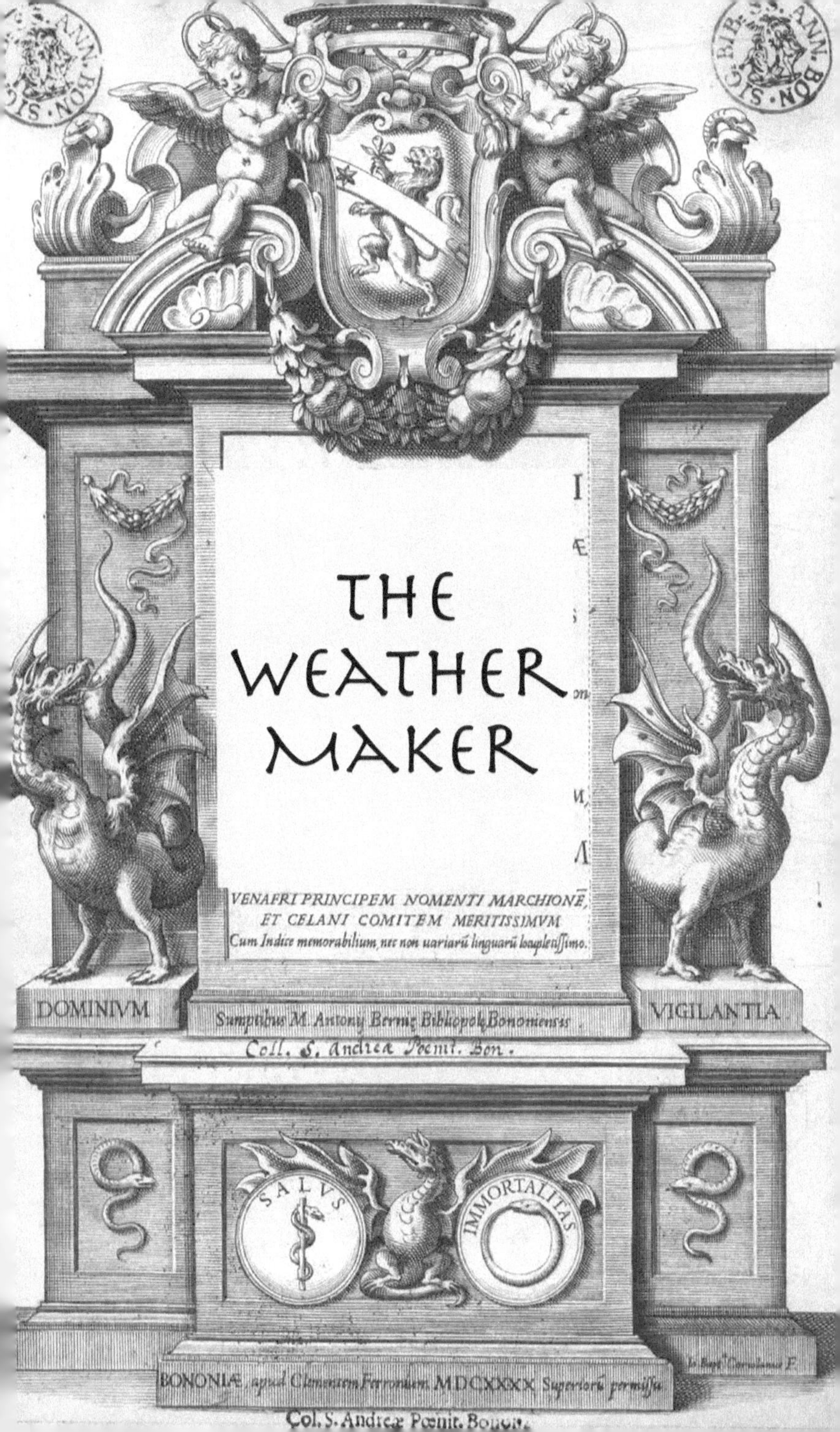
THE
WEATHER
MAKER
VENAFRI PRINCIPEM NOMENTI MARCHIONĒ,
ET CELANI COMITEM MERITISSIMVM
Cum Indice memorabilium, nec non uariarū linguarū locupletissimo.
DOMINIVM
VIGILANTIA
SALVS
IMMORTALITAS
BONONIÆ, apud Clementem Ferronium. MDCXXXX. Superiorū permissu
Col. S. Andreæ Pœnit. Bonon.

He stands in grass alongside the highway, ignorant of the whip of wind thrown by the passage of car after car, the hum and roar of a thousand faceless strangers coming and going, entombed in ceaseless steel.

His pants are pulled high the way old-timers wear them. His shirt is wrinkled but tucked in. He stares up at a sky of uncut blue, devoid of texture or limit.

A man rises from a bench at his back. A bus stop linked to the highway by a turnoff. The man's approach is slow, careful. The man is old, he walks with a cane. The old man stops at the highway's edge and he too looks up at the limitless blue. The old man speaks.

"It's like to rain."

The weather maker takes a gold watch from a pocket. He looks at the time and he looks back at the sky. He does not look at the old man and he does not respond.

He walks west until two city blocks have trod underfoot. An off-white block of a building stands set back from the street. Oversized letters bolted to building face denote the company owning a variety of businesses housed on each floor. Along a sidewalk running past the building's front a few dozen fresh faces hold signs bearing slogans maligning the weather forecast, cursing the local weatherman for the state of the world.

Make Love, Not Drought

Forecast this!

Whoever said Rain, Rain, Go Away needs to take that back!

Mock dissidence, sarcastic picketing. The weather maker stands apart from the marching flock and he watches, he listens as they shout their tongue-in-cheek chants to the world, to passersby, to all. Old protest standards repurposed with a new punchline. Cars honk, people stop to watch. Each in time moves on and among them the weather maker does the same.

The front door is glass set between columns, the building face's only yielding to ostentation. Fingerprints above and below a sign reading PUSH mark the touch of a thousand prior trespassers. The room into which the weather maker steps is divided at its center by a semicircular counter staffed by two receptionists behind which the room trails off into two separate hallways giving visitors the illusion of choice.

The weather maker picks a receptionist using criteria known only to him and as he steps to the counter he locks eyes with this stranger offering to him a smile polite and genial.

"I'm here to see Art Sebastian."

She nods and she goes on smiling and on a console tucked onto the counter's inner shelf she types something as she asks if he's a relation, if he has an appointment. The weather maker turns his face away but his eyes move back to find hers. He tells her no, though to which question his response is addressed he does not say. He tells her the man's forecast is wrong. He says it again.

"I want to let him know his forecast is wrong."

She lets out a quick laugh but he remains placid. She looks at the other receptionist and she looks back. She asks his name and he gives it to her. She asks him to wait a moment please and he does so. She types and she hums to herself. Her eyes on a computer monitor. She only looks up when a man with a large neck and a security badge appears from one of the hallways. The sentinel takes the weather maker by the arm and he speaks with an authoritative air.

"Okay, come on."

The weather maker stiffens and he twists away but the sentinel holds on. It is here he begins to shout. He says the forecast is ruining lives. He says the man's ignorance is poison. He goes on ranting, spittle flying. He says all the things voiced by the marchers outside but his sermon is earnest and brimming with fervor. Lobby folk stop. They freeze, they stare. A woman puts a hand to her face. Someone drops a phone. The weather maker shouts still. He blames them each one. He blames their enabling. He writhes in the grip of the sentinel and he goes on shouting, stopping only when a hand slaps him across the face.

They hold him in a conference room. He sits unspeaking and when two uniformed policemen arrive he is unspeaking still. The policemen exchange pleasantries with the security sentinel and they gather the facts of the weather maker's outburst and with this done they return to idle talk. The weather maker does not look up and he does not speak and soon he is being led from the building.

He sits uncuffed in the back of the patrol car. His gaze faces front, watching the city's unrelenting onrush. Halfway through the trip, in a gentle voice, almost a whisper, he begins to speak. He talks of the wise, the soothsayers of old. He talks of village elders, those keepers of knowledge known for their vision and foresight, revered. He invokes the Farmer's Almanac. The policeman in the passenger seat nods now and then. The driver looks at the weather maker in the mirror. As they pull to a stop at their destination a single raindrop smacks against the windshield.

The weather maker sits on a bench beside a man in a suit chained to the seat's scarred arm. Years of etchings, meaningless leavings, memories. The man in the suit stares at these. The weather maker looks ahead at nothing.

People talk. Officers, others. They discuss him but do not speak to him. They talk of his rant, sometimes interested, sometimes joking. They talk of calling an evaluator, a doctor. The talk moves on, the gossip shifts course. He is not booked and no one is called and in time the weather maker is turned loose.

Traffic buzzes and barks with the start and stop of passing lives. He stands back, face upturned as he waits for the bus. A deep gray has bloomed above. He goes on this way until the squeal and sigh marking the trundling bus's arrival.

People watch the approach and recession of block after block or they hold bright devices in hand, scrolling and swiping and leaning close like lovers. The weather maker looks ahead. He listens to sounds beneath the surface, the quiet hum of the world. Hands on knees, back stiff. Jaw clenched at what he hears there. When the bus comes to his stop he is already standing, he is already moving.

Darkened spots along the sidewalk fade where the touch of furtive droplets are being soaked into the hot pavement or eaten by the wind, the sun, the day. The weather maker walks on until he comes to stand again among the faux protest and its chanting sarcastics. He listens with hope. In time he joins in. They laugh, they chant louder still. He talks, he shouts. He recites the crimes of the forecaster and they dance along to the tune of his preaching. Above and below the world begins to grow with darkness. He tells them he's faced the man before and he will again. With their help he will again. They march, they dance. He stands in their center, roaring his fire into the blackening sky. They march and stomp and they scream along with him, holding picket signs like clubs as the rain begins to fall.

MORNING
STOCKTON
VENAFRI PRINCIPEM NOMENTI MARCHIONĒ,
ET CELANI COMITEM MERITISSIMVM
Cum Indice memorabilium, nec non uariarū linguarū locupletissimo.
DOMINIVM
Sumptibus M. Antony Bernię Bibliopolę Bononiensis
VIGILANTIA
SALVS
IMMORTALITAS
BONONIÆ, apud Clementem Feronium. MDCXXXX Superiorū permissu

There is no order here. Aged tomes wrapped some in leather, others paper, brittle with years, lie stacked or arranged along shelf after shelf with no sign of rank or sequence. Their covers run the gamut; names typical, pulled from best-seller lists of the last half century or more, others arcane and bizarre. Some have no names, no titles, lettering worn away by years or their names never known at all.

Howard stands spellbound, gaze upturned to this wall of possible worlds. The noise of the room and rooms around recedes as he looks not at individual volumes but at the sum of their reality, at the monolithic structure they together create. Music pulses bass-heavy tremors in foundations, the melody's subtleties eradicated by walls and by force so that only a pounding vibration pumps like the heart of the house. People stand gathered in chattering bunches in this room, in every room. Upscale clumps of humanity, ties loosened just enough. A woman cackles at a joke, her laughter eaten whole by the permeating sound. Her dress hugs curves, a red number clinging tight as she squints eyes, bares teeth, a silent grimace of uncontained mirth. She spills a drink as she laughs. No one seems to notice. She breaks away from her assemblage, careening lost through the room until drifting into orbit around Howard, focused on his focus.

A fissure exists in the bookcase edifice, a single square of emptiness among the gathered books, one volume missing from the otherwise perfect structure. It is this hole that draws Howard, a visible blemish in near flawless chaos. The woman sips from the drink in her hand, glass half empty.

"There's a party going on."

He blinks, leans away from the bookcase, unaware until now that he'd been leaning in.

"I'm only here for my boss," he says, waving a hand in no particular direction. She responds with some party pleasantry, eyes wet, cheeks flushed with a mild drunk. Howard looks past, misses her eyes, the pleasant musk coming off her in waves, his notice consumed with a scan of the room.

A man sits on a plush sofa, cushions wrapped in red velvet. A book is held open in his lap. He is a piece dislodged from the order of the room, his clothes showing none of the upscale flash of the other partygoers. The suit of a working man hangs from limbs, fabric thick and color faded. Work boots marred by wear and life. The left eye droops from some long-ago wound. An immaculate part divides a slicked, expensive haircut, a single consent to an inner vanity. He reaches with gloved hand for a glass on a faux-classic steamer trunk fashioned into a coffee table. Shakes the glass, finds it empty. Slow dawning, face puzzled as he looks up from the book. He closes it shut, places its weight on the trunk with care. A cocktail napkin protrudes from its middle where a page is saved. He and his glass are gone from the room in quick, focused steps.

Howard is drawn to and hovers over the book, the makeshift table, bent double, hands clasped at his back in curious pose. The book is a swollen thing, brittle and misshapen, pages made wrinkled and bloated by some long-forgotten calamity. Howard reaches out, a delicate touch turning page after page until he reaches the napkin at the book's center. A photo of thin children with blank faces looks out of the page. Ancient sad eyes set deep in every face. The photo is very old. Its grim details take up most of the page. The caption reads *Stockton Fair, 1898.*

Nothing in the photo looks much like a fair.

Howard thumbs through pages, stopping on nothing in particular, letting attention wander across words or illustrations without context. Maps and clippings are printed at random. He turns to the cover.

An Annotated History of Morning Stockton Township.

The spine is slick and unpleasant. He runs a finger along the surface. It feels almost wet. He sits down.

"I got one for you, too."

Red dress, back from wherever she'd gone. She pushes a drink across the table, raises another to her lips. She leans over, a shadow falling on the book. Howard takes the drink.

***

He's awake for minutes before he knows where he is. Eyes blink, squint at sun filtered through diaphanous curtains, something lacy and thin.

Red dress. Her name is Paige. The apartment smells of something sweet, a candle from yesterday or the day before. The room is small, neat but not cramped. Cozy. He rolls over, puts feet on floor, her floor. Last night comes back in flashes. The first drink, talk of her job, something for a lawyer or something in real estate, the second drink, the other drinks, the cab ride across town, pointing out landmarks that don't matter, the walk up steps outside her apartment. More drinks before it all went black.

He dresses as she enters the room. She mentions food. He thinks of calling into work but doesn't. The book falls out of his coat. He stares, uncomprehending. He wraps it again in the coat, an infant's protection against the cold of the world. She hands him a shoe.

She takes him to a pancake place. Breakfast all day. Thin crowd, customers in booths, at tables. Past the breakfast set, too early for lunch. She asks him about his job. He shrugs, says something about research, about making calls, makes jokes about shielding his boss from real work. She laughs between bites of runny egg. She sees the bundle at his side, the coat and its contents, but she doesn't ask about it and he doesn't volunteer.

Conversation stalls. They exchange numbers and she goes. He orders a coffee, and when an hour has gone by he finds himself in the same corner booth. The bundle on the seat at his side sits untouched for the first cup and the second, but when the third comes he is unwinding the twists to reveal its secret. A finger across the cover earns the same wet, unpleasant feel. He opens just the front cover and turns the first page. No copyright, no legal text. Pages turn. Pause on the photo he'd examined last night. *Stockton Fair, 1898.* The vague edge of a building is visible in the background, the photo's only sign of civilization beyond the sad-eyed children. More pages. Text becomes odd and unreadable as English gives way first to a mesh of language unknown to Howard and then to some gibberish, no language at all. Photos become drawings, child-sized skulls with a thin mask of flesh pulled tight over grins. Stockton Fair, 1652. 1508. 1270. The numbers count back beyond reason. Those terrible eyes, empty or sad. Lifeless orbs imbued with some inner horror. He orders a fourth coffee.

***

The office stinks of some plug-in potpourri tucked away behind a desk or a cabinet, hidden and ominous. Even from the hallway it threatens to overwhelm. Howard takes deep breaths, succumbing to the onslaught of scent as he enters. A woman stands talking into a phone. Some unseen someone types in the distance. Sunlight can be seen through a distant window, but none of its heat is felt in this place. Fresh-laid carpet eats all sound of trespass. Howard moves eyes front through a maze of cubicles, encountering no life on his way to a desk and a laptop he didn't bother bringing when last he left. His searches begin with purpose, the book's title or the name of the town. Soon he is grasping, word combinations and dates that have meaning in his unfocused scan of the book's text. Nothing. He watches the blinking of a mindless cursor, waiting for answers, for something, but time rolls away and no inspiration is found. He closes the laptop. A satchel hangs from a tack. He shoves the laptop and bundle inside.

No one stops him or even notices as he leaves the office, satchel in tow. His boss's door is closed and the light is off. The sound of typing has stopped, if it was ever there. The woman on the phone doesn't speak now, only holds the phone to her ear and listens to some noise a world away. The stink of electric potpourri follows Howard back into the world.

***

The bus is late. Headlights appear among passing traffic, a few at first, then more until only one car in twenty moves dark along the street. Howard waits at the stop with the other stranded, these exiles leaning out one at a time as each looks for but doesn't find the looming approach of an elephantine city bus.

Feet tap and some pace along sidewalk damp with mystery fluid and time unspools for minutes into darkness before the late bus arrives at the curb. The few milling travelers enter in a clump and disperse along the seats. Howard flips through pages of the book, looking at maps. Landmarks stand out, trails where highways should be, names of places familiar but wrong. He closes the book and watches the road pass by, shops lit, some not, streetlamps illuminating pockets of world. He touches the phone in his pocket and thinks of calling her, Paige, red dress. He gets off at his stop and goes into his apartment and is still thinking of making that call as he is absorbed by a deep, dreamless sleep.

***

The workday crawls. Howard fills time with fruitless internet searches, grasping for any loose reference to the arcane details he crosses in his aimless inspections of the book's content. Nothing. He makes a few calls, fakes his way through morning drudgery, but by lunch he's slipping out the door.

He doesn't know where he's going when he gets in the cab. A bearded man with small eyes stares into the mirror, grip on the wheel white-knuckle tight. He waits. Howard gives his answer.

The cab pulls to a stop in front of a swollen offense of architecture. The party house. Howard pays in cash and asks the driver to wait. The driver says no and leaves.

Gravel crunches on the walk up the drive, rocks trucked in from some imagined place. He approaches the house with head down, unsure of each step. The satchel hangs draped across his middle, its contents dragging his body down, slowing progress. He mounts steps like a man condemned. Knuckles rap on a thick door, a dense wood that swallows sound. A man appears, opens door without word. His dress is casual, his face ambiguous. He could be anyone.

"Can I come in?"

The ambiguous man eyes Howard, gives no sign that he's heard. Howard goes on.

"I think I left my phone here the other day. At the party. In the library."

The man does not stir, does not blink.

"I was here with my boss," says Howard, embarrassed and unsure why.

The ambiguous man blinks. He steps aside.

Dust swirls in pale light streaming in through long windows. A sunroom. The ambiguous man disappears into a doorway and is swallowed by the vast emptiness. Howard doesn't follow, instead moving through rooms and halls with a vague idea of where he's going. He encounters no one on the way, only drab rooms decorated with forced imitations of intrigue; paintings of stern faces or lifeless farmhouses in a lost time, new furniture stained with fake age.

The library appears. The shelves are as they were, chaos stacked into a wall of knowledge, centuries of thought, the minds of the vain or the mad captured and displayed. Howard stands where he did before, looking up into that jumble, mouth parted, eyes squinting in perplexity or offense, incredulous.

There is no gap in that wall of chaos.

He runs a hand over the covers of books, no one in particular, feeling the presence they together create. The names and covers are an ambiguous mass that could be as it was or could be shuffled, a puzzle undone and reworked, it's impossible to tell. He looks for the place he thinks the hole should be, moving close without reason, names of long-dead authors inches from his face.

"Find it?"

Howard turns. The ambiguous man stands in the doorway, hands shoved deep into the pockets of the dull, unimpressive pants of anyone anywhere. Howard holds up his phone and nods. The man stands, unblinking.

"I'm not sure how to get back out," says Howard.

***

The bus huffs and snorts, makes all the sounds of mythical beasts. The driver listens to earbuds, the bombastic whimsy of a daytime talk show. A passenger thinks of saying this is some kind of violation, but instead he only watches the driver with a seething disdain. The sun is lost hours before its time, replaced with the patter of rain, a ceiling of cloud lording over the world. Howard flips through page after page. Lines stand out, vague references to the fair, to a figure intertwined with the festivities, a centerpiece figure spoken of in ominous reverence. The bus pulls over. Howard looks up, unsure how long he's been reading. This is not his stop. He closes the book anyway.

Crawling discomfort rides over Howard. He turns. A man is looking his way, a familiar man with a drooping left eye. Howard recoils. Was he on the bus before? Has he been here all this time? Howard changes seats, moves to the front of the bus. He gets off at the next stop, miles from home.

Full dark, rain pelting the awning he steps under, the sound it makes an oppressive presence that crowds in on all sides. He dials her number without a thought for what he's doing. She picks up on the second ring.

***

The swirl of thick, cloying incense looms heavy in the air. Her skin is flushed with drink. She sips and sips again as she listens to the things he has to say. He talks for ten minutes, twenty minutes, doubling back on points he himself is too baffled to let pass with only the one viewing. As the story plays out she offers an incredulous stare, nodding at times, always sipping.

He pauses for a beat, breathes in, out, drinks from a bottle of something dark. She cuts in.

"The guy was on the bus."

"He was on the bus."

"The guy from the party."

"Yes," says Howard.

The incredulous stare remains fixed on him. He looks around for help or for escape, but there is nothing and so he only sits. She speaks.

"Are you screwing with me?"

He pulls the book from his satchel and places it in her lap. She opens to a page at random. A rough sketch of a man with a wild beard and hollow eyes sits among the text, looking out of the page. Paige laughs, a wild sound billowing forth in drunken guffaw.

"Someone should go find this place."

Howard leans back, unsure what she's saying.

"It's not real. It's not a real place."

She looks up to meet his eyes, a guise of solemnity washing across her features.

"That's what makes it fun. Like jumping headfirst into a dream."

He places a tentative hand on the book and draws it slowly back. He closes its pages but does not put it away, only holds its weight in his own lap, a hand on that slick, unsettling surface. Paige speaks into the silence.

"It's a nice thought, though."

She holds the drink to her lips, a coy smile peeking out over the edge of the glass. Her lips appear wet with the vestiges of drink as she speaks.

"Don't you think?"

***

The phone is ringing. The landscape of an unfamiliar ceiling is the first thing Howard sees as he opens his eyes. He grabs the phone. A display reads WORK in bright block letters. He doesn't answer.

Sun splashing onto the room says late morning. An unbroken stillness gives away Paige's absence. Howard is alone here. He sits up, mouth dry, takes a pull from what's left of the bottle on the nightstand. The laptop is open, a website offering affordable bus fares to anywhere in the country. He scrolls and types, filling in his info for a ticket, thinking he's kidding even as he does it, and he drinks and he laughs and when a phone begins to ring he turns it off.

***

The bus is stuffed with the blank faces of strangers. Howard sees none of this, his attention taken fully by the book in his lap. Hollow eyes of a bearded man look out of the page, their pull compelling, fascinating, an energy there that will not be resisted.

An elderly man in the next seat smiles over at Howard, this young man with his nose in a book. He nods with earnest approval.

"Where you headed?" asks the elderly man.

Howard takes a swig from the bottle secreted away in his satchel, not looking up. The book has all of him now.

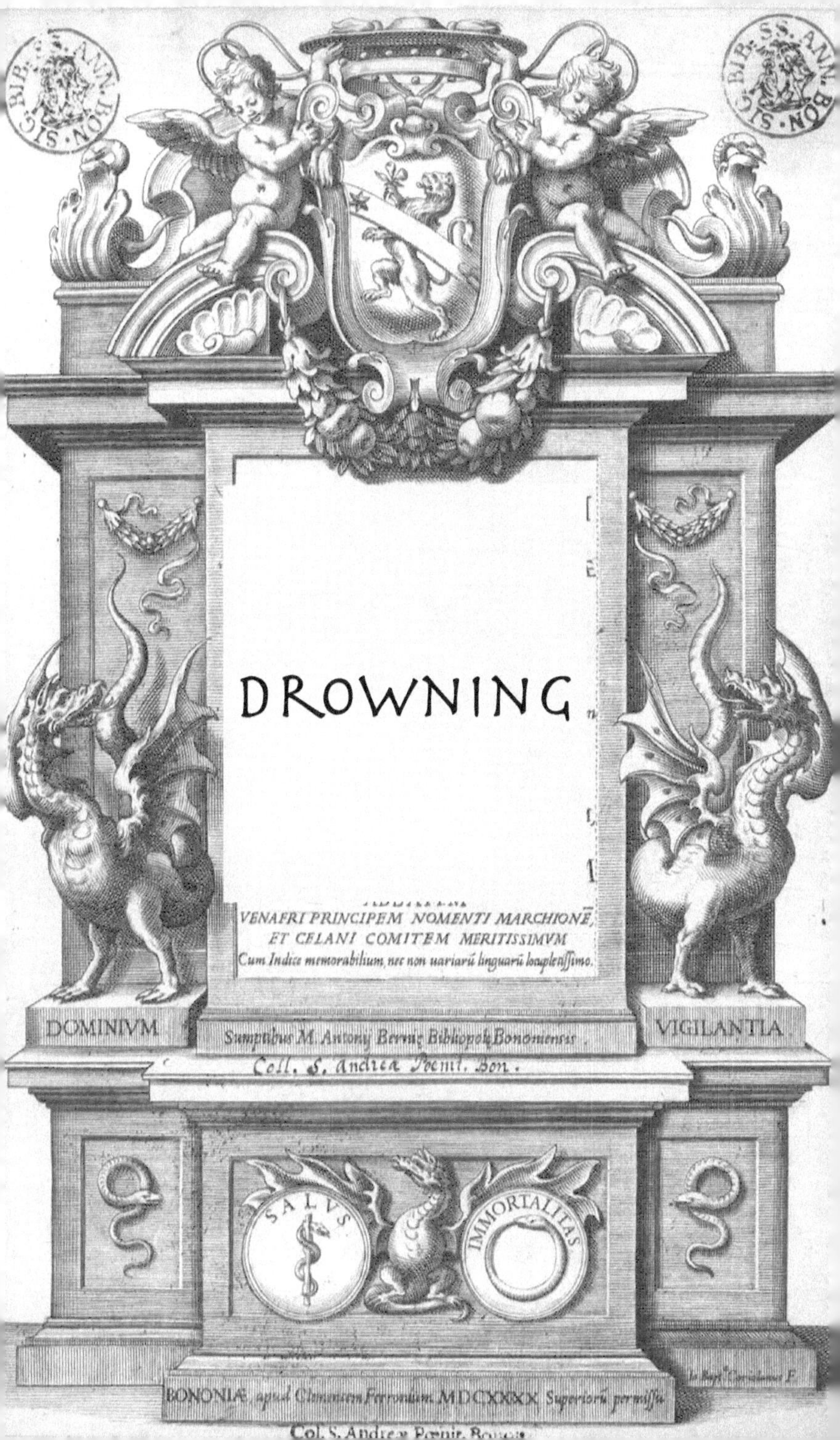

DROWNING
VENAFRI PRINCIPEM NOMENTI MARCHIONĒ,
ET CELANI COMITEM MERITISSIMVM
Cum Indice memorabilium, nec non uariarū linguarū locupletissimo.
DOMINIVM
Sumptibus M. Antony Bernię Bibliopolę Bononiensis
VIGILANTIA
Coll. S. Andrea Poenit. Bon.
SALVS
IMMORTALITAS
BONONIÆ, apud Clementem Ferronium. MDCXXXX. Superioru permissu.
Col. S. Andreæ Poenit. Bonon.
SIG. BIB. SS. ANN. BON.
SIG. BIB. SS. ANN. BON.

The pool doesn't need cleaning. It doesn't need anything. The pipes have ceased their flowing and the waters have all drained away. What remains is a concrete hole.

She sits along the laminated tongue of diving board outstretched over the void. The glass in her hand is held but only just. She leans across legs folded underneath her body and she gives in. Her body hitches, her face is more grimace than frown. Anguish. Her sobbing comes from someplace deep, primordial. A rending of soul.

There are signs of what is lost. A skimmer lies in the grass. A notebook is tucked beneath the deck chair where he lounged. His shirt still sits in a heap on the chair's striped fabric. His shorts are still somewhere upstairs.

She drinks from her glass and for a moment she calms, but it is a fleeting respite from the horror of loss. From a bottle thick and brown she refills her glass and again empties it but that respite isn't there, no solace does come. The poolboy is forever gone, and though she now drowns in a flood of tears the pool from now on will remain lifeless and dry.

SIG. BIB. SS. ANN. BON.
SIG. BIB. SS. ANN. BON.
THE RAILS
VENAFRI PRINCIPEM NOMENTI MARCHIONĒ,
ET CELANI COMITEM MERITISSIMVM
Cum Indice memorabilium, nec non uariarũ linguarũ locupletissimo.
DOMINIVM
Sumptibus M. Antonij Bernię Bibliopolę Bononiensis
VIGILANTIA
Coll. S. Andrea Poenit. Bon.
SALVS
IMMORTALITAS
BONONIÆ, apud Clementem Ferronium. MDCXXXX Superiorũ permissu
Col. S. Andreæ Poenit. Bonon.

The old names don't fit anymore. Hobo, tramp, vagabond, drifter. Simon comes to the yard to sit among the beached railcars rusting and grown over every one and he listens as Walter goes on about the days when those old names still had some kind of meaning beyond flavor.

Employees tolerate Walter. Security armed with flashlights and looking for vandals, clerks come over from the depot or the exchange to smoke or to nap or to have a private moment alone or together. They know Walter is in here somewhere among the maze of hulks, an old man smiling over some memory pleasant and free.

The yard is surrounded by miles of fencing but holes show in places, in places lengths have fallen away to lay flat in dust or in gravel or among wild grasses. Simon enters through any of these and each day he finds Walter sitting in the open door of a rotted railcar or on the stump of some tree or other cut away decades gone by to make way for this graveyard of steel and years.

Simon eats his lunch and he shares it with Walter, half a sandwich or a sliver of melon, an egg boiled hard. The old man eats and he talks with no rush in unfocused bouts, wandering through aisles of memory and pulling down finds along the way. He talks of men dead ten years, twenty years, longer, their stories all that's left, a vague immortality, some growing still, the story taking on an air of legend as its facts are stretched a little with each telling. Their stories are his now, the last man, the wandering figure left to carry these tellings to those that would hear.

And stories they did have. Of their travels, of the things they did, their many lives lived hard and lived fast. And other things. Other stories.

They each on their own made the claim, to have seen the thing on some night in some city, Tucson, Chicago, Atlanta. They describe it as an it or as a he but it is the same in every telling. The suit a deep blue and filthy, the thing's flesh the pale blue of fish belly or corpse. It hums a little tune in the dark and it takes its pick of the riders arranged about in the car and it does devour the flesh and meat of man, the organs, the life. It dances with its pleasure and its bare feet blacked by filth or by tar or the coals of some true hell do move with a rhythm at ease and joyous.

Walter offers up these absurd fables of the rails with a smile. He'll tell the same version of some man's encounter twice, three times, savoring the details as if it is some delicacy he has only now come upon. When Simon asks if he's ever seen the thing Walter demurs.

"Oh now, that was all so long ago."

He drinks some but he is not a drunkard. He goes up into the woods most nights to sleep. He laughs when Simon asks if it is because the thing might come around when the sun goes down but he does not say no.

They say the thing whispers to himself in a tongue foreign to any land of this world. They say when he speaks to the men who shrink and cower in steel coffins streaking down endless miles that it is not with that heathen tongue alien to all sanity but with a voice subdued and polite, the voice of someone known since forever, an old friend, a voice heard in childhood dreams or remembered from the impossible past, dating to the womb, dating to before. They've seen him, every man, when a train car passes with one door pulled wide and his form framed in a moon silver above, that hole in the night sky. They say he's a childhood nightmare come back to haunt these men lost and running, souls come untethered and left to drift to the ends of the Earth, men whom no static point can any longer hold.

When Simon asks why those old days are gone and the men who lived them gone and the names and the stories they together make all gone too the old man looks away and he sits still and so quiet for some time and he is thinking or he is trying not to think when Simon speaks up again, now asking if the men were afraid of that creature, a joke maybe, his smile almost eager, but Walter returns to the moment meeting Simon's gaze and now in the old man there is visible a deep sadness that though there before had until this moment remained well masked.

"I don't know," says the old man.

The moon has rejoined the sky when Simon walks the quarter mile through fence and ground stone and track after track to the active line where shipments of all manner of thing pass daily or they stop for a time between where they began and where they will meet their eventual fate. He looks into an open container and then into another. Voices collude somewhere nearby but they are muted and without consequence. He is here now, in a story of his own making. He is a legend come to life, those long-dead men renewed in just his walking this place, their world returned. He smiles up at the silver moon. When he hears the clank of metal as a line of cars begins to pull away from this world and race into another world impossible to know unless it is lived he does not stop to think or consider but only slaps his palms on the floor of the open car and boosts and leaps and then rolls across floor and lies prone and elated for a full minute, overcome, still grinning the simple grin of a child as he rises and stands and wiping hands on pants begins to contemplate the future.

SIG. BIB. SS. ANN. BON.
SIG. BIB. SS. ANN. BON.
IN LOVING MEMORY
OF
PATRICIA FLOWERS
VENAFRI PRINCIPEM NOMENTI MARCHIONĒ,
ET CELANI COMITEM MERITISSIMVM
Cum Indice memorabilium, nec non uariarū linguarū locupletissimo.
DOMINIVM
Sumptibus M. Antonij Bernię Bibliopolę Bononiensis
VIGILANTIA
Coll. S. Andreæ Poenit. Bon.
SALVS
IMMORTALITAS
BONONIÆ, apud Clementem Ferronium. MDCXXXX. Superioru permissu.
Col. S. Andreæ Pœnit. Bonon.

All of this is wrong. The day is clear, it's bright, colors vivid like a painting, like a cartoon, ethereal and perfect. Dreamlike.

The girl, from her perch on the bridge, turns to look. She's a line in the distance, a splash of movement too far off from the slow approach of Henry's boxy old sedan to matter much, but he sees her, he registers the presence of another soul in this unreal afternoon world. He sees the turn of the head, the look over the shoulder, and he sees her step off the bridge, leaving him alone in this world once more.

He stops the car in grass just short of the bridge. He doesn't think to shut off the engine and a saccharine pop tune goes on playing on the radio, fading away as Henry runs stumbling downhill to the river's edge. The body lies unmoving on rocks worn smooth by time a dozen feet from the water. Eyes open, limbs and neck twisted. Henry pats his pockets but his phone is not there. He looks back up the hill and he looks at the body. Assorted items are scattered around the mouth of a bag. Gum, pens, ID. He upends the bag but no phone falls out.

He makes his way up the hill, sometimes using hands to stay upright, running, climbing, and the phone is there, it's on the driver's seat. He dials and he speaks frantic words to a dispatcher who with professional calm says they're on their way, they're on their way. She tells Henry to stay on the line but he does not hear, he is already gone.

Nothing has changed at the bottom of the hill. He sits down on the rocks and he waits with her. He looks away, embarrassed, and he looks back. He takes up her ID card. Local address and a fairy tale name, Patricia Flowers. He sets it back in her bag and he scoops up the other items and then he has nothing to do with his hands so he lets them fall to the ground at his sides. He begins to weep.

The sirens are still far off. He wipes his face on his sleeve and he looks at her again. He reaches out a hand to close her eyes but he hesitates, he pulls it back.

He moves up the hill slower this time but still he reaches the top before the first car arrives. A tall cop steps out. He says something but his words are eaten by the screams of an ambulance that skids to a halt in the street. He repeats himself.

"Where is she?"

Henry points and the cop walks off in that direction, followed at once by two men in white uniforms who burst from the medical van. Henry waits by the cars. He sits in his driver's seat and shuts off the engine. A bell goes on pinging. Henry closes his eyes.

Someone is clearing their throat. The tall cop stands just outside the car with another officer, a shorter man with a square face.

"Come with me."

Henry follows the officers to the hilltop overlooking the river.

"Tell me what you see."

Henry looks down the hill and he looks at the tall cop.

"I don't understand," and, "Where is she?"

The tall cop eyes Henry.

"Yeah," he says.

They question him by the cars, the tall cop does, the shorter cop does, then another man in plain clothes, detective. The paramedics watch and they whisper back and forth and they laugh. They get a call, they leave. The officers talk amongst themselves and then with the detective. The cop with the square face goes to Henry.

"Do you know what it means to file a false report?"

And

"Are you on any medication?"

More like that. It goes on and on but they do not take him in, they do not charge him with anything. When they are gone he sits behind the wheel in silence.

***

The ceiling wavers, shadows passing through one another, joining and separating, an ebb and flow of darkness. It takes the shape of faces and creatures, first forming and then dissolving each disparate form, the idea of a form, never holding one shape for long.

Henry has not slept. He watches the ceiling and the dance of shadow thrown by tree limbs swaying under night winds' caress. The window is open and the night is cool. A dog is barking, ceaseless repetition of the same sound, bored, perfunctory claps. The shadows sway.

Now it's a road, now it's a bridge. Henry closes his eyes and sees her face and he opens them again. The shadow is a face. Henry climbs out of bed.

A screen glows, a computer hums. The whir of a fan. Henry's face is a pale mask, blue, gray. He types in her name and he searches. Thousands. He scans the features of strangers. Social networks, news clips, articles going back decades. She is not among them. His Patricia Flowers is not here.

A phone rings. He looks at it, watches it. He picks up the receiver on the third ring.

"Hello?"

"You're up?"

Henry doesn't try to hide his sigh.

"Hi, Avery."

"Can you come over?"

He looks at his wrist for a watch that is not there, sarcastic. He feels guilty even though she does not see.

"Yeah. Yes. Give me a few minutes."

She is quiet and then she agrees and she is gone. He puts the phone down and wipes a hand across his face, pushing away sleep that was never there anyway. He stands and he stretches. He slips his wedding ring onto his finger before he leaves.

***

Smoke curls and the air is thick with stink. Vanilla, maybe. Cloying. One stick of incense is going but she lights another. She blows across the end glowing orange and she watches the air swirl. Her pants are loose cloth, soft. They hang low on hips. Yoga pants, pajamas. The abstract tendrils of her tattoo are visible just above the waistband. Her hair is a tousled halo, dark and perfect. She isn't wearing her ring.

"You want a drink or anything?"

He closes his eyes. The chair he sits in is plush, thick, a field of cloth to sink into. He takes a deep breath.

"I'm okay."

He hears her circling, a change in the air, something. He doesn't open his eyes.

"I'm glad you came. Today was hard."

He waits for her to elaborate but instead she shifts gears.

"We're not getting back together."

"I know."

She begins to speak but loses focus. The air moves, her presence drifting about the room. She mutters something unintelligible. She's drunk or she's stoned, something. Narcotized. Henry can hear the smile in her voice when she speaks clear words again.

"You can stay tonight if you want."

"Okay."

"Did you have something you wanted to talk about?"

The room is quiet. The air tastes of a candy sweetness that chokes. He inhales a slow breath and holds before letting it out. He takes in another filled with her air. She's moving, she's close.

"I can't think of anything," he says.

***

The unrelenting barrage of beeps is a noise foreign to him. He jumps in place, covers thrown to the floor. Heart races. He smacks her alarm with a palm until it ceases its wail.

He drags himself to the bathroom and empties his bladder, half asleep still, one hand on the wall. He stands in the quiet a moment and knows she is not here, has already left for work. His sigh is heavy. He flushes the toilet.

***

Rows of desks are empty and the quiet goes on for miles. Screens are hot and bright, time stopped. Coffee steams in cups where it's been left. A television whispers somewhere, volume turned low, banal musings imbued with the unearned menace of a hushed tone. Henry falls into the chair behind his desk. His eyes are unfocused, face turned up, looking off to nothing at all. A phone rings at another desk. No one picks up and after a minute it stops.

A door at one end of the room opens and a woman enters. Twenties, ruddy cheeks. The slap of each step echoes. She holds a paper plate as she walks, steadied by both hands, plastic fork tucked between two fingers. Her path takes her toward an office but she veers off when she spots Henry. She smiles as she approaches him but he doesn't notice. She forks a bite of pastry into her mouth, a treat colored an unnatural red, slathered in frostings of various colors. A candied letter A sits pressed into the surface. The woman chews a moment. Henry sees her, he nods at her. She smiles again.

"Aren't you hungry?"

He looks at a clock on the wall.

"It isn't time for lunch yet."

She squints and she stares.

"Are you okay?"

His eyes slide down and away.

"I didn't get much sleep."

"Yeah?"

"I saw a woman jump off a bridge yesterday."

"Oh my god."

He looks up at her again.

"Yeah," he says.

She shuffles weight from one foot to the other. She waits for more and when no more comes she cannot control herself. She puts a hand on Henry's shoulder.

"There's cake downstairs," she says. "Charlotte's retiring."

***

Blues and greens and reds, platters of designer cakes surrounded by celebrants and chatter. Strangers partake. Unfamiliar faces from upstairs, from downstairs. Henry wades into the crowd but the tables are packed on each side with bodies. He turns one way and then another in search of necessaries, plates, forks, but he finds nothing. He mumbles words, excuse me, excuse me, but no one moves, no one helps.

The ruddy-cheeked woman emerges from the stairs. She moves through a crowd that parts at her approach. She stops at the table and cuts herself a fresh piece of cake. The ruddy-cheeked woman leans to another of the congregation and she speaks and they laugh. She points at Henry as she talks.

***

Henry's sister pours syrup on her eggs. She nods a lot and she orders a margarita with lunch. Her suit jacket hangs from the back of her chair. She listens as Henry talks and then she eats in silence for several minutes. She takes a drink and another moment passes. Her fork clanks as she sets it on her plate.

"Like a ghost?"

Henry shakes his head.

"I sat with the body. I waited with her until the cops came."

She picks up her fork and she puts it down again.

"You called the cops?"

"I thought they were gonna arrest me."

"For what?"

"I don't know. False reporting, something. I don't know."

"Who else have you told about this?"

Henry shakes his head.

"Did you tell Avery?"

"Not yet."

She finishes her drink and she orders another. She sits in silence until the drink comes. She sips and stares into the distance. Henry pulls her plate across the table and picks at the remains of her meal. He watches as she nods to herself. She leans to dig a phone from a pocket of the jacket on the chairback. She turns back long enough to hold up a finger. One minute. She stands and moves to the bar. She talks to the bartender and she talks into the phone. Lunchtime patrons meander. Talk and music and the hiss of something frying. When Henry's sister returns to the table her mouth is a line. She sets a new drink next to the one she has not finished.

"Do you have insurance?"

"What?"

"You're going to see my doctor."

"Your doctor."

"He's good," she says, sipping her drink.

***

All the doors are open. People sit in chairs or they sit on examination tables lined with strips of paper long and thin. They look at phones or at nothing at all. Old, young, some scared, some distracted. Henry, led by a woman in camouflage scrubs, passes each unbarred entry and pretends not to see. She takes him to an empty room like all the others. Chipped tile, vague floral wallpaper. She throws out invasive questions and she never looks him in the eye. She laughs at something, he knows not what. After several minutes of talk she leaves Henry alone in the room. She does not close the door when she goes.

Someone coughs in another room and somewhere a man is crying. A voice is speaking soft words, tone soothing but the content of their murmur too low to discern. Henry closes his eyes and sinks in a chair. His head rests against the wall. Someone goes on coughing.

"You're seeing things."

A man is there when Henry opens his eyes. Olive-skinned, face round. He's looking down at a notebook, eyes moving back and forth at something there.

"No," he says.

The man writes something in his notebook. He reads it back to himself. His lips move with the words. He clears his throat and begins asking the same questions as the woman in the scrubs.

"Are you on any medications?"

And

"Do you have any allergies?"

And

"How's your sleep?

Henry gives the same answers as before, or he thinks he does. He speaks when he must and he nods at all the right times and in time the man tears off a note and hands it to Henry.

"Take it with food."

Henry says he will.

***

He doesn't notice a change, not at first, and then he does, in the first week, in the second week, after the fact, not a numbness but a distinct estrangement from feelings both tactile and emotional, a detachment from now, walking through a mist.

Henry is at his desk. He's typing, he's nodding but not listening as a woman talks on and on. He's still nodding in the dozen or so seconds after the talking has stopped. Henry looks up. She speaks one word.

"Hey."

She points at Henry's face. He raises a hand to find tears rolling down his cheeks.

"I'm okay," says Henry.

***

Pills rattle in a bottle, in a pocket. Henry pushes open a glass door smoked and opaque and he steps into air conditioning and calm. A woman draped in blues and badge looks up from behind a counter. She offers a smile. Henry's mouth is dry.

"How do you find a missing person if you can't prove they exist?"

She looks around to see if anyone else has heard this but the few faces in the foyer are each of them turned away.

"Is that a riddle?"

Henry swallows and he swallows again.

"I think I need to file a report about a missing person."

A man emerges from a side hall. Short cop with square face. In his hand is a brown sack. Lunch. His eyes fall on Henry.

"Oh hell."

Henry turns.

"I need to talk to you."

The uniformed woman looks at Henry and she looks at the short cop.

"You know him?"

"This is the guy with the ghost story."

"Oh, wow. Oh. The ghost guy."

Her amazement is earnest and without shame. She grins ear to ear. The short cop looses a heavy sigh and puts a hand on Henry's arm.

"All right. Come on."

Henry asks where he's being taken even as he's following along.

"We're gonna go into a room over here and I'm gonna eat my lunch while you say what you have to say and then with a little luck you'll go away and I'll never see you again as long as I live."

The table is dark wood, not polished in years, scuffed and plain but not shoddy in its construction. The short cop with the square face eats with elbows propped on the cool wood surface. Sandwich in two hands, lettuce like lace protruding from the edges of a dress. Henry remains standing.

"This isn't a ghost story."

The cop chews. He swallows a bite before he replies.

"Okay."

He takes another bite.

"I looked her up."

More chewing. The cop takes a drink from a can with an orange stamped into its side.

"You looked her up. How'd that go? We looked her up, too. Your ghost story was big news around here. Our researchers loved it. They went back a century looking for your dead girl. Take a big old guess what they found. Not a thing. Not a thing. Not only has no one by that name either lived or died in this county over the last hundred years, but there is not a single recorded suicide on that bridge."

"She's not a ghost."

The cop sets the remainder of his sandwich down on wrinkled wax paper.

"Then what is it? What was your name?"

"Henry."

"Then what is it, Henry?"

Seconds pass. The short cop picks up his meal and he bites off a large hunk. The sound of chewing is loud in the quiet of the room. He washes the last bite down and he drops each piece of refuse into the paper sack. Henry watches this without comment.

"Well?"

"I have to go."

The short cop laughs.

"You do that, Henry. Put up fliers for your lost ghost. Good luck, Henry."

Eyes follow Henry as he makes his retreat through the lobby but his own eyes remain straight ahead, never meeting the gaze of another.

***

Henry sits on a bench at a bus stop but he is not waiting for the bus. He looks out at the park across the street, joggers moving along a path worn by ten thousand disparate feet, strangers drawn to the same track as those who have come before, men playing chess or checkers, their flimsy boards set atop tables warped and desiccated or the stumps of trees cut down in some other year, long before now. A man sits on a bench not all that different from the one upon which Henry is seated. He sits beneath a tree and he eats a sandwich as he watches the same world Henry sits watching. When he sees Henry the man looks away.

A woman walks by and then she walks back. Runner; the shoes, the clothes. She scans the street, the park. Her hand is wrapped up in a leash, the end dangling above the ground, swaying in the breeze as she looks first one way and then the other. Henry watches this a moment. She doesn't stop her search long enough to see him.

"Are you okay?"

She jumps at the sound of his voice. She laughs and he sits, face unchanged. She holds up the leash with one hand while the other takes hold of the aluminum clasp at the end.

"I broke the goddamn. The goddamn thing broke."

She looks back at the street a moment.

"Have you seen a dog?"

Henry shakes his head.

"I'm sorry," he says.

"This doesn't happen. I don't know what to do."

Her shoulders slump and she drops onto the bench, face turned to the ground.

"Fuck."

Henry nods but the woman does not see.

SIG. BIB. SS. ANN. BON.
SIG. BIB. SS. ANN. BON.
THE
FARMER'S
SOLUTION
VENAFRI PRINCIPEM NOMENTI MARCHIONĒ,
ET CELANI COMITEM MERITISSIMVM
Cum Indice memorabilium, nec non uariarū linguarū locupletissimo.
DOMINIVM
VIGILANTIA
Sumptibus M. Antonij Bernię Bibliopolę Bononiensis
Coll. S. Andrea Poenit. Bon.
SALVS
IMMORTALITAS
BONONIÆ, apud Clementem Ferronium. MDCXXXX Superioru permissu
Col. S. Andreæ Pœnit. Bonon.

Headlights cut the passive swirl of snowfall in the night. He leans across the wheel to see but there is nothing to see. Road, night. He holds a phone to his ear. Now and then he utters a curse, but this is not an angered sound. A voice bereft of spirit trickling words into the moment. He offers up gentle communion and a shared pathos when he does speak but it is the feminine voice on the other end of the line carrying the talk along. He is to listen. He is to hear.

The heat is turned high, turned all the way up. A fog creeps its slow way up the window. He rubs a hand on the glass and the space cleared there fogs again. He listens to her talking. He curses, he says I know. He leans back, he drives with his knees. One hand fumbles with a knob but the defroster does not come on.

When he hits the deer he is looking down. He is driving and then the world is still and he is stepping from the open door into the snow's lazy drift. Between these two moments there is violence and nothing.

He touches his head. Fingers come away wet with blood but it is not much, no pain comes with that touch. He steps to the car's front. A headlight is smashed and dark and another shines the way ahead on empty road. A splash of black marks the snow and a trail of steps and blood lead away to the silhouetted trees at the edge of the world.

He lowers himself back into the car. He turns the key and nothing happens and he does it again. He sits in the quiet. He touches his head again and wipes fingers on pants. He leans and pats the passenger seat and then down to the floor where his hand connects with the phone. He takes it up and presses a button but the fractured screen remains dark. He stares for some time at that inert slab and then he lays it on the seat at his side.

The door groans as he pushes it to its full reach and again steps into the snow. He pulls a long winter coat from the back seat and wraps himself in its bulk and buttons each button with fingers numb from cold. Then he walks.

He sets off in the direction pointed by the headlight's throw. In time that beacon falls away at his back and he is left alone on miles of trek down this lane of cold blue. He shoves hands deep into pockets and later he tucks them under arms. He walks on and on. He does not count the minutes but he feels their passing. He shivers and groans. Steam leaks on hot breath.

A light appears and with each step it grows. In time the shape of a house coalesces around that glow and the light itself is not one but several shown in that old farmhouse frame.

The path he veers onto is one imagined in the field of unbroken snowfall, a loose progression toward that antique structure. Still more time passes in slow churn as his steps drag through mire, but that farmhouse does near, its wellspring of glow leaving nooks of cold shadow like worn stark line in its aged facade.

A man stands smoking a cigarette under the light of the porch. The bleeding man in his coat pulled tight climbs steps of old wood that cry out underfoot. The man on the porch gives a slight nod. His face lets out a mist of steam and smoke. Around his frame is wrapped a thick woolen blanket and from this he puts out a hand. The bleeding man takes it and they shake and the smoking man takes that hand back and adjusts the cigarette perched between his lips and this done he again stows that arm away inside the blanket's warmth. The bleeding man stomps his loafers and clears his throat and speaks.

"I wrecked my car up the road."

The smoking man nods again. The bleeding man says it's cold to be out here smoking and the smoking man says my wife makes me smoke outside. Then comes a beat of mulled silence, and then the smoking man is thumping the cigarette out into the snow, and he is turning, he is saying come on.

"I'll host you here for a bit."

The bleeding man follows along behind his host through a foyer where he knocks feet against door frame to shake loose snow and then on into an inner room where a table is set with two bowls and two spoons and two squat, round glasses. A serving dish sits at the table's middle but a lid opaque with sweat obscures its contents. Beside this is a tray of fat biscuits, a dish of butter, a square bottle of something dark, a long, thin knife.

"Sit, eat. You're my guest."

The guest does sit and the host hands him a cloth napkin and nods and gestures at his forehead gash. The guest dabs at this place and he looks at the napkin's stain. What's left there is all but dried and the wound has turned to a sealed carapace. Still he touches the napkin there again. Then he folds it into a neat square and lays it on the table.

"I need to use a phone. My car."

The host nods. He takes a seat at the table with his blanket still wrapped around him. He takes a biscuit from the tray and tears it open and with the knife he cuts a square of butter that he lays on the biscuit's soft, moist flesh. He takes a bite and chews and he takes another and another and the biscuit is gone. He rubs his hands together and crumbs fall to the table. He stands with slow care and keeps the blanket pulled around his form as he leans and takes up bottle and glass and pours a splash of dark liquid. He leans back into his chair and holds the glass against his chest and says well, he says go on then.

"It'll help with the pain."

The guest says there's really no pain, but he pours a drink and drinks it down and pours another. The host speaks.

"Where were you headed? Before."

The guest sets his glass on the table but his fingers stay wrapped around its form. His eyes remain fixed there as he talks.

"I was on my way to meet my ex-wife. We're supposed to go to a funeral."

"Your people or hers?"

"What?"

"Who died."

"Oh. Hers. Her people."

The host nods. He sets down his glass and takes another biscuit and he holds it in two hands.

"Then why go? Are you still close?"

"I don't know."

And he says it again.

"I don't know."

He pours another drink and sits holding it. The host breaks off a hunk of biscuit and lays the rest on his plate. He puts the hunk in his mouth and works his jaw in slow chew, his eyes loose, looking off to nothing, looking at some faraway thought. When he speaks again he asks the guest who were you doing it for? For your ex-wife? For yourself? It's not for the dead.

The guest looks at the host and looks again at the glass. He takes a long sip. He does not answer. The host nods and he lets the blanket fall from his frame to lay at his back in the chair. His form is rail thin in simple buttondown, wire and muscle under pink flesh. He reaches into a shirt pocket and takes out a ragged pack of cigarettes with lighter tucked in its wrapping. These he lays on the table. The guest's eyes find their way there. He takes a drink, and another. He empties the glass and sets it down.

"Is your wife coming in for dinner?"

The host waves a hand around at nothing in particular. He breaks off another hunk of biscuit and looks at it a moment before he eats it down. A chase of drink follows the bite. Then he leans his form in to the table.

"Did you want to go?"

The guest makes a noise, a scoff.

"Who wants to go to a funeral?"

"Then why go?"

"It's just, you go. It's what you do."

"It's habit. It's momentum. This isn't your anybody. Your ex-wife has a reason to be there, sure. The only reason you're going is because you don't know you're not needed."

"But it's the right thing."

"It's not the right thing or the wrong thing. It isn't anything."

He stops talking and takes a drink and pours full his glass.

"Would you want her people at your funeral?"

"That's not the same at all."

"It isn't the same, that's true. But would you?"

"Some, maybe. Sure."

"Not those. That's people you share. You specified. You were clear, this is hers, not yours. Would it mean anything to you to have her people see you off in the world?"

"I want to say yes."

"Well that's a lie."

The guest shifts in his seat. He puts a hand on the table and then moves it back to his lap.

"I'm gonna call you a car. Okay. Okay, here's what's gonna happen. You're gonna start walking back to your car, and I'm calling somebody to come out and pull you into town, and that's how long you've got. You can go to a funeral and be an accoutrement in someone else's world or you can send your condolences and then go live a life that someday ends with the people you want at your funeral. Those are your options."

The guest flinches and he laughs an awkward guffaw but the host only sits unsmiling. A moment passes in quiet, and then the host is reaching into the pocket of simple slacks, he is setting a phone on the table's face.

"You should get going."

The guest hesitates. The host only sits waiting. The guest pushes off the table to stand and he pulls his coat tight around him. He makes his way back to the door and still the host only sits. There is a creak and then the slam of a door and the host is alone. He takes up the cigarette pack from the table and shakes one out. He lights it and breathes in and he empties his lungs of smoke. He leans back into his chair and crosses one bone-thin leg over the other. He takes one more long draw on the cigarette and lets smoke roll in slow curls around the empty, silent room.

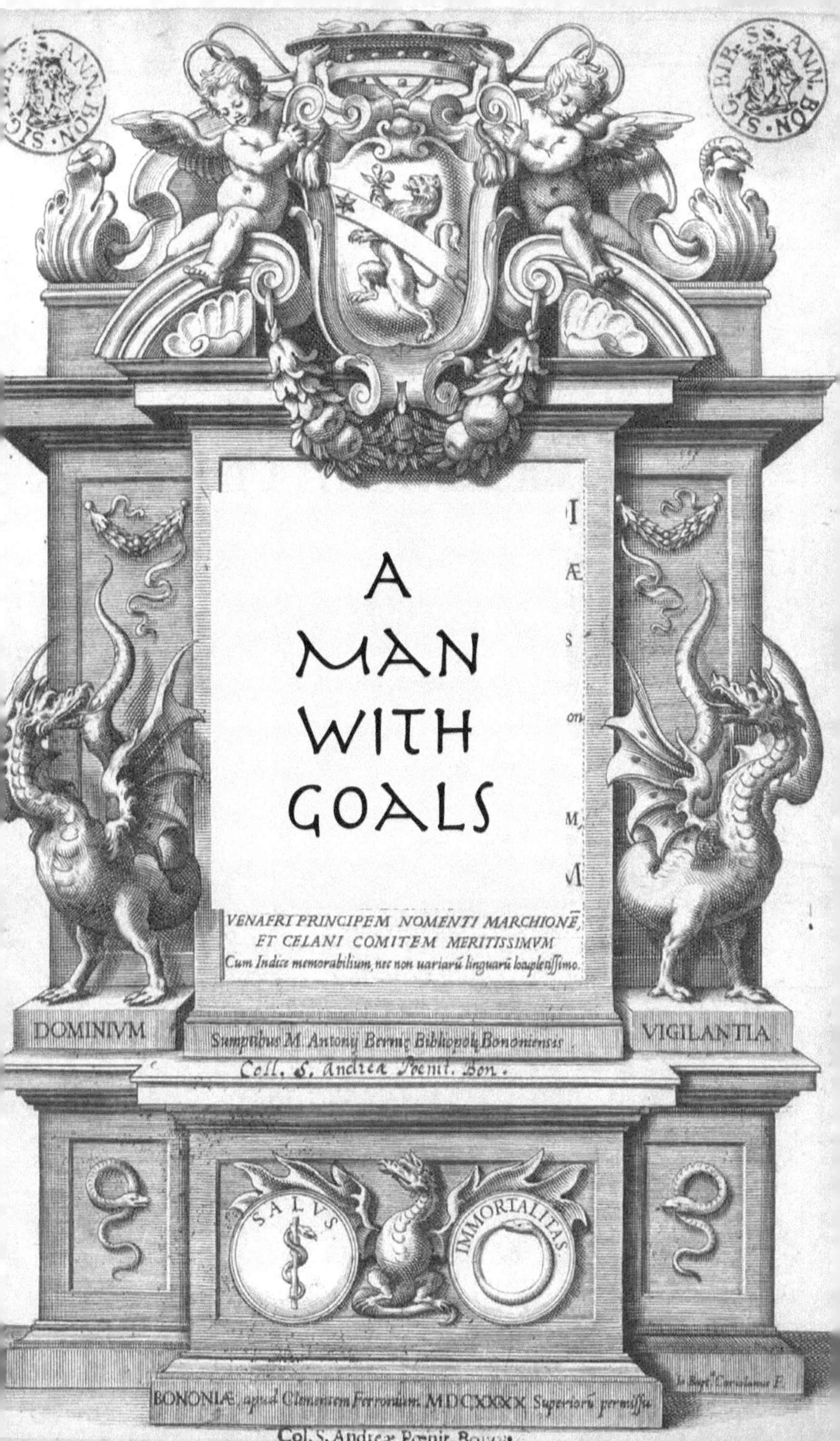
A
MAN
WITH
GOALS
VENAFRI PRINCIPEM NOMENTI MARCHIONE,
ET CELANI COMITEM MERITISSIMVM
Cum Indice memorabilium, nec non uariarũ linguarũ locupletissimo.
DOMINIVM
VIGILANTIA
SALVS
IMMORTALITAS
BONONIÆ, apud Clementem Ferronium. MDCXXXX Superioru permissu

The bus is running late. They wait by the stop, these men, these women. Some look to the sky from which the rain has stopped falling but again soon will. Some look at phones or they look up the block for the bus that has not arrived.

Ephrem looks at the ground, at a pool of rainwater gray with the muck of city sidewalk. He is looking at it still when a man elbows past. Ephrem stumbles, he falls. One knee hits pavement at the puddle's bottom. Gray water soaks fabric. Ephrem remains kneeling. He looks around at faces turned his way. A man among them laughs. He grins at Ephrem, he says be more careful. He does not offer Ephrem a hand.

A grate of tired brakes marks the bus's stop. Doors open with a huff. Those waiting climb in, Ephrem stands and he climbs in. The march between seats has feet clapping on narrow aisle floor with a sound like tap shoes. Vinyl sighs as each rider sits. The doors are closing and the bus is moving.

His pants stick to his leg. Ephrem looks, he stares. He runs a hand along that place, to ring it out or to test the extent of this shame. He goes on staring.

A man takes the seat at Ephrem's side and he offers a hand. He is a well-dressed man but his person is unkempt, face unshaven in a week of days, hair uncombed, standing in places. The hand remains extended and when it is not taken the well-dressed man points at Ephrem's leg.

"Does that piss you off?"

Ephrem doesn't look at the man.

"Leave me alone."

He sits in the moment. When he's ready he goes on.

"Yeah it pisses me off. Of course it pisses me off."

"Why don't you do something about it?"

"Do what?"

"Anything. Hit the guy who knocked you down. Anything."

"He hits me back. What good is that?"

"So it's the consequence that stops you."

"Yeah."

"Didn't stop him from knocking you down."

Ephrem looks at the well-dressed man. He says nothing.

"Is that it?"

"What?"

"Take that part out. Absent consequence to you, would you hurt him?"

"Come on."

"I'm asking."

"I don't know."

The well-dressed man waits. He looks out the window and he is looking out the window still when he speaks.

"Are you a man with goals?"

"What does that even mean?"

"Hopes and dreams and whatnot. You have those?"

"Everybody has those."

"Like what?"

"Success, stability. A big house. What everybody says. You know."

The well-dressed man looks at Ephrem. He talks of decisions. He talks of the will to do things, to achieve things, success in whatever form it may take. A big house, he says, and he laughs. He says of decisions that they are always made, whether we are the ones doing the deciding or not. He says choosing not to choose is itself a decision. He moves his hands when he talks, warding off spirits, pointing to things that are not there. Then he stops, speaking, moving, all. He waits.

"Okay."

"Okay what?"

"Just okay."

The well-dressed man nods. He says okay and he offers his hand again. Ephrem looks at it. In time he takes it. The well-dressed man nods again.

The bus is stopping with its squeal and grind and Ephrem is stepping from its doorway onto pavement. He stands atop a hill looking out over the city below in every direction. The bus sighs and it pulls away. Ephrem stuffs hands in pockets and one leg he shakes to feel the now dry cloth fan the skin there. The bus descends until at hill's floor it whines once more but does not stop. When the truck impacts the bus's side the clap is distant and inconsequential. Ephrem does not look down to see what has happened. His eyes remain ahead. An old growth of foliage has survived here throughout the comings and goings of years, and there in the distance the rooftops of mansions show just above the trees.

MODERN
ROMANCE
VENAFRI PRINCIPEM NOMENTI MARCHIONẼ,
ET CELANI COMITEM MERITISSIMVM
Cum Indice memorabilium, nec non uariarũ linguarũ locupletissimo.
DOMINIVM
Sumptibus M. Antonij Bernię Bibliopolę Bononiensis
VIGILANTIA
Coll. S. Andrea Poenit. Bon.
SALVS
IMMORTALITAS
BONONIÆ, apud Clementem Ferronium. MDCXXXX. Superiorũ permissu
Col. S. Andreæ Pœnit. Bonon.

At first it didn't matter who she called. Old lovers, ex-roommates, the A listings in the county phonebook. She would talk about stories that weren't her own. She would touch herself or she would laugh or cry or both. She would hang up without saying goodbye.

She found Paul by accident. She didn't know his name was Paul but she imagined it was and it was. She said Paul sounded like someone she knew once before but she never knew who that was. She said Paul was nice.

His number was scribbled in a frantic hand on a yellow notepad that cost half a dollar. She called him every day to tell him about every nothing she imagined. She would talk about her day. She would talk about her wants. She would tell her own stories and she would laugh. She would hang up without saying goodbye but she would always want to call back. Sometimes she would but always she would want to.

One day she killed a man. She was driving the speed limit and she had not been drinking. She was not listening to the radio and the sun was bright in the sky. She was wearing her seatbelt.

The first policeman held her away from the accident. He let her cry for a long time on his shoulder. He said to her It's not your fault. It's not your fault. He said sometimes these things happen. His voice was deep and rich and he smelled like her grandfather.

A long time later the officer drove her to her home. He told her to sleep. He said it would be okay and he told her he was sorry. He squeezed her hand and she went into the house.

She had to try twice to dial the number. She had to wipe tears to see what numbers she pressed. It rang seven times before a woman answered.

"Hello?"

She didn't say anything. No one else had ever answered Paul's phone before.

"I can hear you breathing."

The voice sounded almost like her own in a vague way she couldn't place.

"I'm sorry, my brother was killed in a car accident today."

The woman is there a moment longer and the line goes dead. She's hung up without saying goodbye.

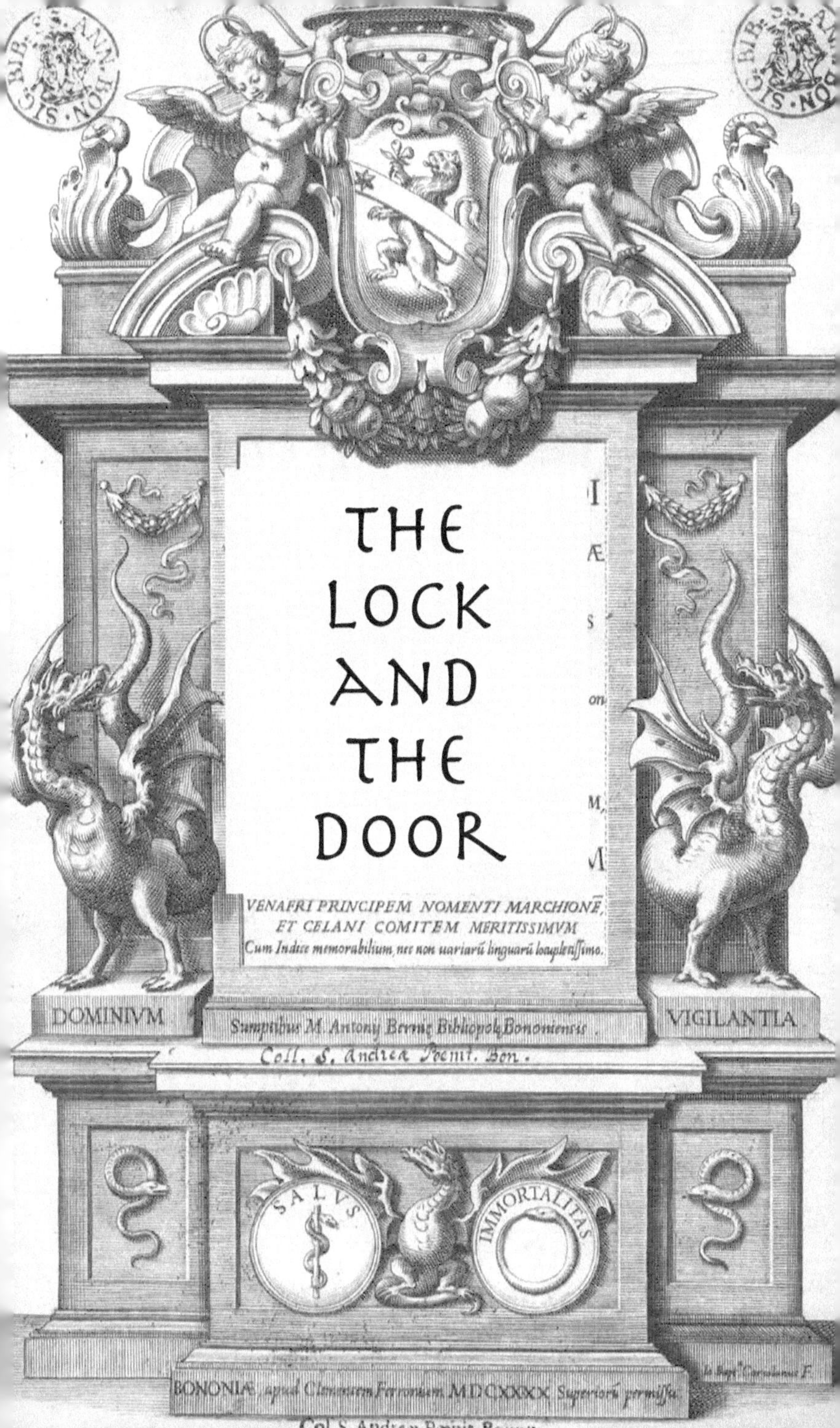
THE
LOCK
AND
THE
DOOR
VENAFRI PRINCIPEM NOMENTI MARCHIONĒ,
ET CELANI COMITEM MERITISSIMVM
Cum Indice memorabilium, nec non uariarũ linguarũ locupletissimo.
DOMINIVM
Sumptibus M. Antony Bernię Bibliopolę Bononiensis
VIGILANTIA
Coll. S. Andrea Poenit. Bon.
SALVS
IMMORTALITAS
BONONIÆ, apud Clementem Ferronium. MDCXXXX. Superiorũ permissu.
Col. S. Andreæ Pœnit. Bonon.

This is an auction, two towns over. Cooper taps a newspaper against his knee as he waits. He looks around at the faces of strangers seated in rows of folding chairs in a high school gymnasium. He listens to their talk but he does not join in. He unfolds the paper and lets his eyes wander over the ad for the auction and he folds it once more. He waits.

A door whines and sunshine enters in a silver haze and through this walks a man in a tailored suit the color of caramel and a straw panama which he removes and holds to his front as he walks. The man with the hat climbs three steps carpeted in felt and locked at the edge of a dais of wooden planks unpainted and unstained. The man stops at a lectern where he drops his hand and raps his knuckles and looks out at the room of faces now turned to look at him every one and this man is the auctioneer.

"Right, then."

He takes up a notebook from the lectern and he turns a page and reads to himself what is there and then he turns another. When he speaks he explains to the room how things will go, that items will come up in an order chosen by whimsy and bidding will go on as long as it takes until all items have gone. He gives his talk in a voice jovial and dipped in the color of an accent it hides but for the soft end of a word out of every dozen or so, too little to discern, the sound of some place other than here.

A tractor sells, and a car of a model not made in years. Some items sell in lots which have no description beyond a serial number and dimensions, size or weight. When a house comes up it sells well below market value, and when another does it does the same. Cooper bids on each but each time he is shut out. The third house to come up is the Francis Top house.

"This one's furnished in full, so if you like throwing out somebody else's stuff, here's the one to bid on."

There is some laughing and the auctioneer nods and then he is reading out the house's pertinent facts, the address, the size, and there is a note and that note reads that the house was built by Francis Top.

Cooper is the single bidder.

***

The keys come to him unlabeled. Cooper goes room to room in the Francis Top house and he tries keys in doors and cabinets and in latches on trunks and each time one turns with a satisfying click he takes a pen and a strip of tape and he labels key and lock both. A ring full of them, jangling as he walks. Some keys stick in old locks but each does in time turn.

A string hangs from ceiling that when pulled draws stairs leading up to darkness. He climbs until he stands on level ground once more. He breathes in the scent of years. When he is ready he makes his way to a wall and from there to a window shrouded in folds of thick wool which he pulls aside and anchors on a protruding nail. Sunlight touches this place. He steps into that diaphanous curtain of dust and warm haze. The outline of a wardrobe does coalesce in a corner. Cooper steps near and turning again to the light he searches his ring of keys for those still without a name. He tries one which does not fit, and he tries one which fits but does nothing. He tries another that clicks and throws a bolt that frees intimate banality these decades locked away. A suit jacket hangs from a peg, a tie loose but tucked knotted into suit collar. Pants shaped in neat fold lay on a shelf next to a wallet and items necessary for the purpose of smoking. Cooper takes up the wallet and he goes through its compartments but there is nothing there to find. He shuts the wardrobe doors and adds label to door and to key.

A rolltop desk is a shape in the dark. He runs fingers along its curved face until the cleft of a keyhole is felt. Again with the keys in the light. One small among the rest fits and it turns and he's rolling up the cover, he's staring into the dark. He closes eyes and opens them again but no shapes take form in that black. He waits. He puts both hands on that old wood and he hefts and drags until light falls onto the desk in its frame. More seconds in the dark bring a chair of simple make. Cooper sits. Dust whirls in the sun. He scoots close and on the desktop lie blank pages and an inkwell long dried. To the right there is a shelf and on this shelf there is a line of envelopes filling one end to the other. He takes one up and with great care he pulls a letter from its casing. It tells details of some minor political squabble from more than a century prior. He returns it to its place and pulls another much the same. And another, and another. Each offers thoughts on subjects with reference loose and vague and with context in many wholly lacking. Their placement along the shelf tracks in more or less chronological placing through years 1890 to 1912. He puts these things back as found and he shuts the cover and he labels key and lock but he does not lock the desk back or move it from the light.

Time is spent feeling for lightswitch or pullstring or lamp but none is found and his search is abandoned. Downstairs he checks the keys. Three remain without label and after a walkthrough of each room they remain that way still.

He finds the door on the third day. He opens windows to let in sun and air and to cleanse rooms of a staleness too entrenched to dust away and when pulling back curtains one reveals a door without adornment save a lock, the gray, metal housing of which is in the simple shape of a gaunt face, keyhole in mouth. Cooper retrieves the ring of keys. He tries each still lacking name but the lock does hold. He kneels, he looks close. The keyhole shows only black. He does not go outside, he doesn't have to. He's been all around this house, and though this is an exterior wall he knows there is none matching it on the other side.

***

The tomb is beneath the town courthouse. He searches online and he confirms with a tour guide and there is no doubt. The guide unlocks an iron gate and he leads the way down a set of stairs into catacombs cut into bedrock. The guide wears a waistcoat and bowtie and he speaks in the whispers of a man afraid of disturbing some long-held peace. He points out the tombs of town founders and swells whose doings offer subtle reverberations in the fabric of township life still. Each door is like that of a prison, thick, iron, forbidding. The guide says behind each door is still more stairs and beyond the stairs sets of rooms for family and what counts as family and these bloodlines are forever sealed in these vaults.

Cooper follows and he listens and when the talk turns to the structure of these tombs and their sealing he asks just what that means. The guide raps a hand on a door. He points to a keyhole where he's knocked.

"The families get them. The keys."

"You said the families are buried together."

The guide nods. His eyes blink and blink again. His smile is sardonic.

"We don't all die in time to make the list."

Cooper asks to see the tomb of Francis Top and the guide's smile spreads.

"The sage."

"I guess."

"That's what they called him. The mayor did. And the judge. The guy was Rasputin before Rasputin."

Cooper says oh, he says he understands, though he does not. He follows the guide along the hall deeper into the catacombs and around a corner where he then stops at a door like any other save the ornamentation housing the lock, a face, gray, gaunt, with keyhole in mouth.

Cooper takes a step back when he sees. He asks the guide if he has a key for this and the guide says no, he repeats himself to Cooper.

"The families get the keys."

"Then what? What if they move off? What if they die off?"

"Then there's nobody coming to visit the dead anyway."

Cooper looks at the door and he looks at the guide.

"Does Francis Top have any living descendants?"

The guide taps on the door and he says oh yes, oh yes.

***

The walls are painted blue and the hallway is empty. Cooper walks past a station manned by no one. He rounds a corner and walks on and at another empty station he stops and waits. He leans across the counter and says hello but no one appears, no one comes running. He moves on. The first door he comes to he knocks at and when no one responds he opens the door. A woman sits at an unshaded window. Her hair hangs down her back in silver strands. She turns to look at Cooper and then she looks away.

"I'm looking for Gideon Top's room."

She does not turn again. Cooper goes back to the hall.

An orderly pushes a cart hauling some sort of mechanical device, a thing with gears and tubes and a readout showing numbers. Cooper asks his question again and the orderly points out a door in the distance.

"Fourth on the right."

Cooper thanks the orderly and makes his way to the door. He knocks and a rasp of a voice calls for him to enter. He does. Inside the room wary eyes look out of a face carved in years, a man slouched and thin draped in the clothes of a man he once was, fabric hanging loose, bunched in places.

"Gideon Top?"

"Sure. Who are you?"

"I bought Francis Top's house."

The old man looks at the floor and he looks back.

"My house."

"What?"

"That's my house. They took it away from me because the county says I'm an old man. You believe that? What right do they have to take a man's home?"

"I don't know. I don't know anything about that?"

"You come here to gloat?"

"I didn't."

"You come here to spit on a old man? Rub his face in it?"

"Mr. Top, no. I came to see if you had the key."

The old man recoils.

"What key?"

"There's a door. The housing for the lock is just like the one on your family tomb downtown. This historian told me they give the keys to the families."

The old man moves to rise but his body does not cooperate and he falls again into his seat.

"Who are you? What are you doing here?"

"I thought you might have the key."

"Fuck you. Get out of my room."

"Mr. Top."

"Get out."

The old man begins to scream, sometimes words, sometimes only noise, rage and fear and noise, and Cooper is running, he is running from the room and from the screaming and from the old man and the thought of the old man, all thought of the old man.

***

It takes him time to make up his mind. He moves forward like he's going to do it but he stops and he thinks. He is unsure still. But in time he does commit and when he does there is no more hesitation, there is no more thinking. Cooper jams the crowbar in the narrow seam between door and wall and he heaves. There is a groan of things coming apart and then a dry crack, and at long last Cooper finds what is beyond the locked door.

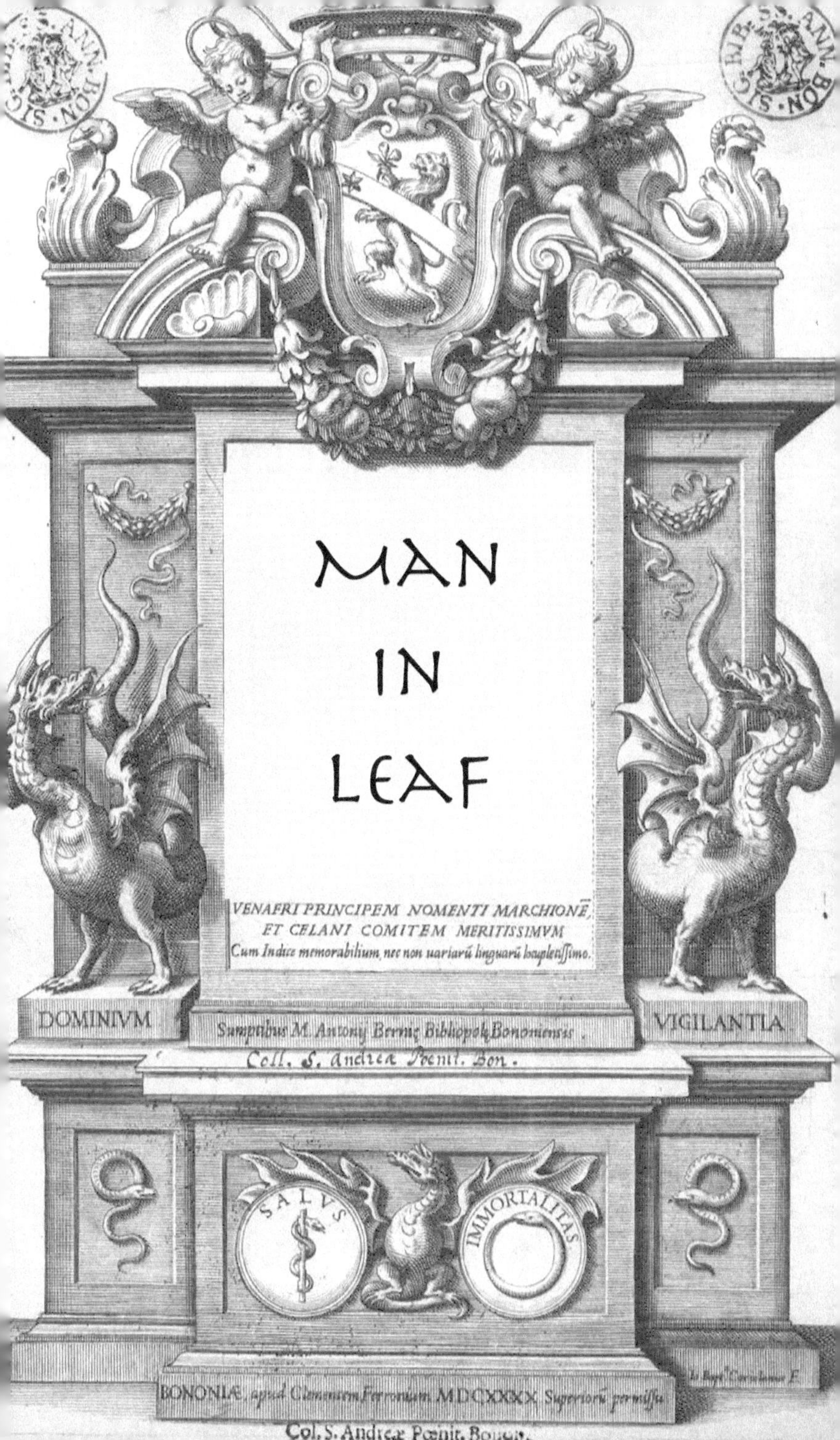
MAN
IN
LEAF
VENAFRI PRINCIPEM NOMENTI MARCHIONĒ
ET CELANI COMITEM MERITISSIMVM
Cum Indice memorabilium, nec non uariarū linguarū locupletissimo.
DOMINIVM
VIGILANTIA
Sumptibus M. Antonij Bernię Bibliopolę Bononiensis.
Coll. S. Andrea Poenit. Bon.
SALVS
IMMORTALITAS
BONONIÆ, apud Clementem Ferronium. MDCXXXX. Superiorū permissu
Col. S. Andreæ Pœnit. Bonon.

The leaves are everything. Vines are only suggested, a line of shadow the span of a hair while leaves cover canvas from end to end in a tarp of greens and cold blacks. There is a tree, or there is the idea of a tree, a hinted depth underneath the skin of leaf facade. Layers real and imagined.

The man isn't there and then he is. Nelson stares and he waits and out of the sharpening contours appear arms, torso, head. Semblance of a figure. As Nelson watches the painting the man reveals himself.

"It's a metaphor, you know."

Nelson takes a step away from the speaking stranger but he is reluctant to move further from the painting.

"Is it?"

Something to say, a toss of words. The stranger nods and points. He looks to make certain Nelson is seeing.

"The leaves are the world."

Nelson mouths a noncommittal okay.

"The lines make the leaves."

Parting words as he drifts along on the current of crowd, swept away. He grins like a monster in the dark and is gone.

A voice speaks up from nowhere, the voice of anyone. "The artist is here."

The wine is warm. Its label bears the name of a celebrity. Nelson carries a glass but doesn't drink. A placard beneath a painting is carved with words. *Man in Leaf*. Nelson runs a finger along letters sanded and smooth. One spot missed and sharp, a splinter for someone somewhere, later, not now.

"You can't buy it. It's already sold."

He slouches, canting to one side, his strings cut. The artist. The tart on his arm looks at nothing. Her eyes flutter, open but only just. Narcotized or asleep.

"Where did you get the name?"

The artist runs his tongue across the rim of a glass flask. He drinks and he smacks his lips. Stink of caustic flood. Rubbing alcohol, gasoline.

"I think the name speaks for itself. It just came to me."

One hand twirls air. Punctuation for a thought. He looses a garbled laugh, a thick, wet noise. The tart sways in time to a tune in her head.

A fan enters the artist's orbit. He wants an autograph, he wants a photo. He talks of obscure works and they bond and they laugh. The artist performs. He takes a drink and creates this moment. A woman looks at the photo and she looks at the room. She speaks in a whisper.

"I don't see the man in the painting."

Someone laughs and then someone else. They share looks and nods and they drink and they hum with a collective energy. Mood moves electric though the gathered congregants. The place is alive with faces and hands, eyes of influential ghosts studying the curves of framed accidents, their fingers ignoring signs asking that the paintings not be photographed, that the sculptures not be felt up.

"Who are you?" asks the artist as he climbs deeper into a bottle. His tie is loose but not loosened, pulled with care to its calculated informality by a publicist not here. Nelson's tie is green.

"I work here," says Nelson, lying.

The artist scoffs, a kindergarten noise jumping out of his mouth. Spittle stays on his lips. He doesn't wipe it away.

A screech flattens the room's humming talk. Fire alarm. The threat of sprinklers and ruin or fire and ruin, doom in every path. Hands carry flutes of spirits through each exit.

Sidewalk gathers the awkward chatter of exiles. Should we go? What about the after-party? The street reeks of exhaust and perfume and a vague, uncertain horror. Nelson's eyes slip slowly shut and the air begins to taste cleaner, more real. He breathes in until it hurts, until he might pass out. Someone laughs about a barren painting. Greens and blacks, a mess of vines and leaves. Simplistic, empty.

"It's a metaphor," says a man in the crowd.

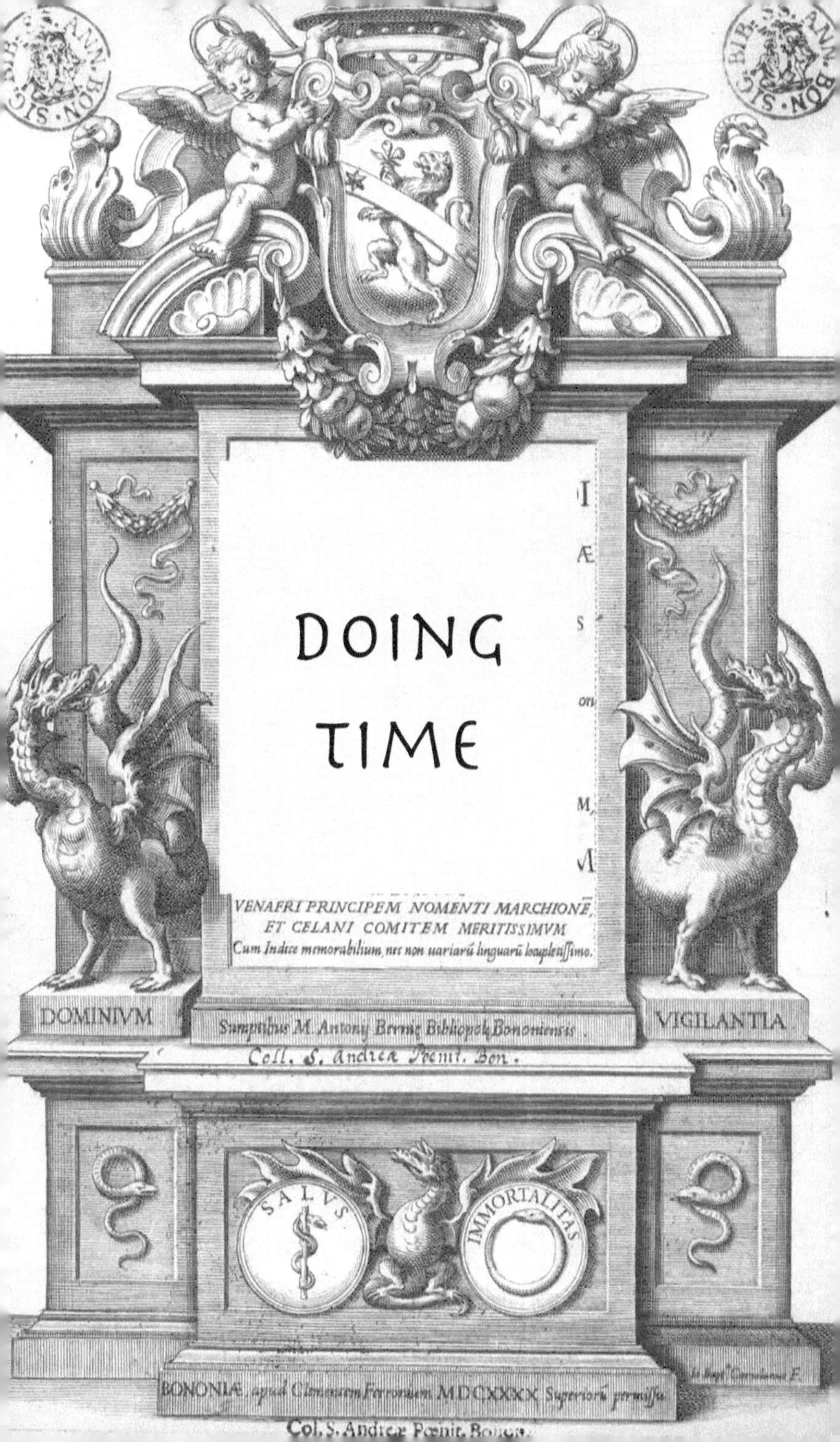
DOING
TIME
VENAFRI PRINCIPEM NOMENTI MARCHIONĒ,
ET CELANI COMITEM MERITISSIMVM
Cum Indice memorabilium, nec non uariarū linguarū locupletissimo.
DOMINIVM
VIGILANTIA
Sumptibus M. Antony Bernię Bibliopolę Bononiensis.
SALVS
IMMORTALITAS
BONONIÆ, apud Clementem Ferronium MDCXXXX Superiorū permissu

1.

He is a salesman, he tells people, and it's more or less true. He tells them his name is Gray, when they ask, which it isn't, and they rarely do. He says the past doesn't matter and he leaves it at that, but it does, it matters, and it is always there, some shred poking out, a thread waiting to be pulled and its haunted treasures unfurled for all.

In the front hall, in a closet, behind the coats and things, boxes containing unimportant memories, there is a bag filled with money. Bundled bills in mostly large denominations. A case like a doctor might have in some bygone era, the kind that might be dragged from house to house as such an archaic medical practitioner checks mending bones or as he might listen to strained, tubercular lungs. The tools of this trade are gone, replaced with those bills in small stacks, the bag clasped and hidden, tucked behind the mildewed baubles of life.

The house is a dry, quiet thing tucked in among other houses of its antique epoch. These few square blocks of yesteryear rest in a sea of suburban boredom, houses and homes born fully formed in long rows, each cast from the same horrific mold, not like these creaking husks that were here before and will be here, reticent and stoic, long after the others have spun drunken and canting to dust. He rents the house with cash for almost nothing. Its rooms are furnished with musty flea market finds and a hodgepodge of kitschy relics. Lamps crafted by bored geriatrics in community classes, tables cobbled from foraged refuse by aspiring or failed artists. And a painting. *The painting*, he calls it, because it has no name, or if there is a name it is not written or saved, is lost to existence and its fickle memory. A field of tall grass, bent in the hand of wind, each brushstroke there to tell its story. In the middle distance is a figure, a dark line with hat pulled low, the suggestion of a man there among waving stalks. A fixed touch of structured lines at the horizon could perhaps be a farmhouse, remote and inconsequential.

He sits looking into the painting some nights, those nights when he can't sleep, when he knows the stranger is coming.

He is a salesman, and the boon he peddles to those who ask is the smiling lie of his own persona.

2.

The fire in the east is a new day's start. Mowers start early, big industrial monstrosities that rattle windows in distant frames and stink of gasoline for two blocks, three blocks. Sprinklers will be on in a half hour, automatic spritzes mimicking a light morning rain, but for now there is nothing. Later there will be crowds, kids playing on playground swings, jungle gyms. Nannies will read paperbacks off to the side, some talking with each other, sharing pedestrian tidbits about their lives, their employers, others only sitting with vacuous stare, waiting for something else. Old men will sit at tables, wooden park tables or cut stone slabs, cheap cardboard games set out, chess or other finds. The old men smoke, tipping burnt ends in the grass or just letting lengths of dead ash hang from the end wedged between bent, gnarled fingers as they contemplate moves. People will eat lunches, accountants and lawyers. Scorekeepers with paper bags. Sandwiches wrapped in plastic, white bread and a single piece of lettuce with cheap meats between. Meals for the frugal or the dieting. Sometimes a single piece of fruit.

This will be the world, but it isn't the world yet.

Gray sits with eyes closed. The bench at his back is damp from morning dew. Hands rest on the thinning knees of once fine slacks. The seams of his aging three-piece are loose, fraying or frayed from countless years of faithful service. Dapper in a past life. Lines in his flesh tell the story of years. Eyes move behind lids, free roaming an unknowable world. Lips slightly parted, he breathes in morning scents, fresh-cut grass and wind and sun, earthy fragrances both sweet and bitter. He sits in this fashion as all around the chaos swirls. The brazen roar of the mowers progresses inward, their bulks moving first in stripes and then in chaotic swirls unrecognizable to logical minds, blades chopping grasses to nothing in a mad dance as the vibrating behemoths abandon their coordinated march and lunge with greedy intent at the naked remains of uncut pasture. Their chorus rises and nears until all else has vanished and only the unremitting tumult exists in the world, is the world entire, the tremble of ground and pulsing air replacing all that had once existed.

Soon they too are gone.

Gray opens his eyes to find a lifting blue tone in the sky. The fire has subsided, appeased. A woman in muted sweats jogs along a sidewalk that rims the park. She sings every third or fourth word from a song playing in her head. She turns a fleeting smile to Gray as she passes his perch. He returns the kindness, but she is already gone.

***

Diner noise makes background music. The pleasing chime of silverware on glassware, the idle chatter of people and lives, cars somewhere in the distance. Gray sits at the counter, always at the counter, a glass of water in a chilled glass placed atop a folded napkin. The water is complimentary, handed out to anyone who wants, but he pays a dollar whenever he orders.

"It's only fair," he tells whoever is working the counter; the fat man with the spacey glaze in his eyes, the young woman who used to manage a bank, who knows how she ended up here, the geriatric miscreant with the sly look, sometimes others. There is a turnover rate, a come and go of crew to man this ship, but Gray is there, always there at his post.

He holds the paper folded at the crease, eyes moving with meticulous care over article after article, no hurry in their appetite to devour the world and all its secrets one blurred line of ink at a time. Others tap keys, look with deep longing into glowing screens of phones, play games clutched in bent hands. All around patrons are enveloped in media, a bottomless bombardment of the instant update. The only newspaper is the one in front of Gray.

The man across the way leans forward, hands on counter. He squints. Eyes move side to side, up and down, minute spins and turns as he examines from his distant seat the crossword that lies opposite whatever day-old intrigue has Gray bewitched.

Gray's eyes continue their steady march across the page as a terse, measured query finds its way from his lips.

"Help you with something?"

The man across the way points one finger at the paper.

"I see that when you're done?"

Seconds go by, maybe a dozen, not many more, and the droning march of eyes on page ceases.

"You can see it now."

Gray folds the paper over again, hands it off to a passing waitress with a point and a nod and she turns, not pausing, only setting the paper in front of the man across the way before she moves on, lost in a sea of eggs and pancakes, orders and checks.

The man across the way looks over the crossword, flips to the front, goes back to the crossword. He meanders, a man unsure of his place, taking in bits of stories but never staying for the full show. Gray watches, sipping water.

"How would you know?"

The man looks up.

"What?"

"If I was done. How would you know?"

"With the paper?"

Gray doesn't respond.

"You'd get to the end."

Gray handles the man's response, tasting its intricacies in his mind while his face remains placid. Eventually he speaks.

"That's fair."

The man waits for there to be more, but no more comes and he goes back to mercurial perusing of yesterday's news. Eyes widen by something they find. Gray sets down his half empty glass as he watches the man read. A waitress stops by the man, asks a question.

"Anything else, Chester?"

Words go unheard as the man reads. Chester. His clothes are sharp, the pressed attire of a man who should be somewhere right now but isn't. Dark shirt, collar buttoned, no tie or coat. A thick neck protrudes from that collar. When he speaks there drifts an accent afloat somewhere just behind the words, the faint touch of somewhere else. It is the sound of a city on the coast, some hard place that has exiled this wayfarer, doesn't want him back. He watches the room even as he reads, but he doesn't take notice of Gray, and he does not see Gray watching.

A waitress stops by the place where Gray sits on most days, maybe a waitress that has served him a hundred times before. She smiles, pleasant but distant, and pours from a pitcher to fill his glass just as many others have, as they always do. No one remembers a time before Gray came to this place.

***

The air in the room is thick with must. Mildew, dust, older things permeate the stillness, rings of barely visible miasma wandering the ether. Gray sinks low between the arms of the chair. The painting presides unprejudiced over stark drama not yet played out, that aged canvas waiting for something more. Gray looks into that unchanging image, the unwaving grains and beyond that a world unknown. He longs for sleep that doesn't come, not believing it will but still wanting, unable to give up on the possibility of something more.

A knock comes at the door. A long breath in and a slow breath out and he answers with the same feigned lack of feeling he's practiced for years.

"Hello, Gray," says the stranger.

3.

A woman sits in a sun-filled diner with pen clutched hard in slender fingers. The pen moves at a determined crawl across a bent page of lined paper. Care is taken with each word, the plot unfolding for her as she goes along. A note or letter, maybe a list of items to pick up on the way home. The mystery of the mundane. Gray watches the pen's movements from where he sits, his newspaper folded over and forgotten in hand.

"She somebody you know?"

Gray turns. Chester sits across the island from him, a vaguely interested look on his face as he waits for Gray to answer the question. Gray holds up the paper, offering this solemn token as reply.

"No, thanks," says Chester with an unwarranted shake of his head. He looks first at the paper still hanging in awkward expectation and then at Gray whose face gives nothing away. "Can I ask you something?"

Gray gives only the slightest shrug as he puts down the paper.

"How old are you?"

Gray doesn't blink or look away, doesn't move at all. He breathes in and holds, breathes out and speaks.

"How old do I look?"

"Upper forties, maybe a spry fifties. Like that."

Quick nod from Gray.

"Okay," he says.

Chester sits a moment, a thought not quite ready to come loose. And then it does.

"You know anybody who died?"

"Everybody does."

Chester looks away, considering the point or just waiting.

"Yeah."

Noncommittal. He focuses on the paper in front of Gray, letting his eyes have someplace to be. Gray looks back, but Chester has receded and whatever thought was there is now obscured by too much time. Gray turns to the woman, who has folded the piece of paper and stuffed it into an envelope. An address is written there and covered by a torn wedge of masking tape. A new address is written on top, but the letters from the old show through as ghosts of another place. She asks a man working at the counter if they sell stamps here, but she knows they do not. Gray watches as she walks out the door, stuffing the envelope into a hip pocket as she goes.

"A friend of mine died and no one called. I had to find out about it in the paper."

"Don't read the obituaries. They're only ever depressing."

"I don't," says Chester.

A moment becomes a minute as such utter pause holds the room in thrall, as if all the chats and all the phones and the typing and eating and living look around to see if something is amiss of which they've only just now become aware.

The moment soon passes, the vacuum left behind quickly filled with the return of a forward-leaning, gregarious Chester.

"You always wear that suit," he says. "Nothing changes."

Gray stares back without real commitment.

"Chester," he says, and waits. "Always has very little to do with me."

A moment passes by. Gray turns to the window to let his gaze move over his own reflection, but the sun is so bright and where his reflection should be there is instead the world still moving on the other side of the glass.

***

A hatter in suspenders measures the head of a shriveled elderly man. The hatter digs through a case, a finger running over fabrics one at a time, searching for something or simply feeling, experiencing. He flips through a book, pointing out patterns and styles and chatting up wants and tastes with the elderly. The elderly nods or stares, smiles at times. His eyes close when he smiles and long teeth show white between thin pale lips. The hatter falls silent, contemplative, steps through a corner door and is gone.

The shop is a cozy burrow here, a den of open space surrounded by walls hung high with hats of all ilks, but beyond the door exists a cold wasteland of pre-cut suits lined in row after row of heartless, unloving racks. Other rooms lie along that open room's walls, brief oases in a fashion desert, quality booths adorned with works by artisans who ply their trade in unlabeled obscurity, artists destined to be forgotten. Tailors and their underlings mend or cut fabric, prepare for greatness that which is as yet only potential, all this in the confined nooks of outlying regions in this warehouse of garmentry.

Gray sits waiting for the hatter to return, waits for the hatter to finish with the elderly before getting to him. Each man sits in identical chairs, each seat suffering from the same forlorn degradation, years of asses worn into the material. The elderly flips a hat in his hands, a dented felt thing, dark brown and not at all like the others in the room. The hook from which it is taken shows stark among the others left behind, the wall of hats with nothing inside and in that one spot a dead space, blank among the mounds of cloth.

"Do I know you?" asks Gray. He looks into the elderly as he speaks his question, unsure if he's asking because the question might collect a yes or if he's merely tossing away time as an exercise in frivolity.

The elderly goes on turning the hat. He speaks.

"I want this hat."

His eyes take in the worn but sturdy cloth. Bent fingers move along the crooked length of brim that leaves the shape off balance and odd.

"I want to take it with me. I want this hat, but it's old, it's ragged, dog-eared, and there exists a point when you can't go back to those things once you've left them. You follow?"

Gray nods, not sure if he understands, only wanting the man to go on.

"I haven't owned a nice hat in a long time. In a lot of years. It's hard to find a nice hat. One that feels broken in the first time you put it on, a natural extension. You ever been in prison?"

The question sits a moment, Gray not noticing or not committed to answering, finally speaking in his own time.

"Define prison."

The elderly spreads cracked lips and emits a sharp, abrasive sound, a rasp that could be a laugh. A touch of that sound remains in his voice as he begins to speak.

"Fair enough. I have. I've been in a prison. More than one. No fine hats in prison. Sometimes there's a hat, nothing quality. Nothing a man should find himself wearing."

He looks at the walls which surround. He doesn't wave a hand or even nod, and Gray does not turn from the dry husk of humanity sitting before him.

"You don't talk much."

Gray says nothing.

"I met a man like that once. Not a talker at all. I was in a place I didn't know, wasn't there long before I got moved on, but I heard stories. About this guy, yeah?"

His mouth opens to go on, but breath stops, held in. The hatter enters at a professional glide. From a pocket is produced a length of string. Old markings from a pen show where something was once denoted at various spots along the thread. The hatter wraps this around the skull of the elderly, taking care with casual aptitude not to move a hair from its fated place. He marks the position at which the two points cross behind the head of the elderly. His gaze catches Gray for only a moment before graceful steps draw him once more from the room.

The elderly looks at Gray, acknowledging the inevitable continuation of his own story. Gray only looks back, awaiting the flood of words that the elderly is about to loose.

"He worked in the prison library. Old guy, very old. One of those polite-to-nod-to kind of guys who looks like he'd be mean if you knew him. Like he's quiet for a reason. Guys told stories, they called him the librarian or they called him the old man. If he had a name of his own I never did hear."

The elderly stands and stretches as if he's been sitting for days. The bent felt hat is placed with unsettling tenderness on the now empty seat. He moves around the room in slow circles, examining the uncalculated varieties of headwear found on each wall.

"Legends are like that, you know? The little truths that hold them together get mixed in with the mortar, the bullshit of it all. You could ask anybody there, nobody could tell you how long the guy'd been around. You get me?"

He plucks a hat from the wall, one among many, an old-style derby, that doesn't match, barely fits, should look silly but somehow doesn't. Cloth so black it looks wet. He runs a finger along the brim, tips the end when he gets there with a smile.

"They said that old man had always been there. An institution unto himself. As much a part of that spot as the prison built around him, a thing occupying a particular point in the universe and could be found nowhere else, never. Not ever."

A slight gap appears in his words as he notices the dented hat where he left it. He retrieves it with one hand, holding it out before him, looking for something or just looking, then pulls the arm in, the hat resting against his chest as he finds the dangling strands of his stray musing.

"Bunch of bored criminals telling stories. I like that story. I like it because it sounds like someone didn't think it through, yeah? How is this old guy always there, always older than anyone else? Wouldn't there be records? Paperwork showing when he arrived? Say he's got a life sentence, even that shit can't go on ad infinitum. What'd he do, this librarian? I like it because it sounds like bullshit. It sounds like bullshit, but there's just something there, something about the thought of a kindly old man handing out books with that hard, mean look, in the way he never blinks, how he gives a smile that's wrong in some way you can't wrap your head around, there's something in the way the mind can touch that story and immediately want to wave it away that I. Just. Like."

That rasping laugh comes again, a dry, ugly thing.

"Also, no," says the elderly.

"No what."

"No, you don't know me."

The elderly drops the dented hat in Gray's lap. He does not pay for the derby he wears as he leaves. When the hatter returns he finds each chair empty.

***

It's the end of the universe, thinks Gray, as he stares into the dense and endless black coffee he didn't order. This is what the end of the universe looks like. The edge. This is what the edge of the universe looks like, he thinks to himself, corrects himself, but the difference in phrasing is negligible. He slides the cup to the side but doesn't send it back. He puts a dollar underneath and looks away, tries to forget it's there.

She walks by. She, he thinks. Her. He could give her a name, make one up, pluck a string of letters from the heavens and apply their delicate frame to her, present it to her like some unwrapped, unplanned gift, but he prefers her as she is, an ethereal creature passing rapidly by in a world parallel to his own, a momentary near collision of dimensions that cannot be fully comprehended until the moment is already at its end, and maybe not then. Probably not then. She reminds him of someone or she reminds him of the idea of someone, of the projected understanding of a personality from his past.

She sits at the same table as before, placing in front of her a sheet of paper or several sheets stacked, extras in case she makes a mistake. The pen moves with delicate flair, the intimacy of familiarity, moving along its fluid thoughts to reach a point that lies somewhere in the middle distance, an idea half seen and not yet understood, the pen and the woman wielding it reaching out together toward a conclusion to some private moment they and they alone share.

The crisp sound of ruffled paper shakes the moment apart. Chester holds a newspaper, page folded to a crossword. The tender chime of a bell marks a door's opening. The noise of the world breaks upon the shores of diner walls, a scant second and then it has passed, the door shut once more and the world held at bay. A stranger crosses the room, a smiling relic in a fine coat and hat. He leans across a counter to share a secret with a waitress. She smiles and turns and has forgotten him entirely.

Gray pales in the afternoon sun that finds its way into the room. Spots of color show the heat under skin. He slips another single under the coffee he didn't order. The cup is cold. He puts down a ten on top of the singles.

***

A knock meets the door, cordial raps that wait for an answer, not retreating from the peace that follows.

Gray once thought of the thing on the other side of that door as the old man, as time has gone on he's forgotten why. He once called it the visitor, other names that didn't fit. Now it is only the stranger.

He opens his mouth to say something, some frail acquiescence, acceptance of entry, but he exhales only barely contained defeat with no words on that breath. He crosses the room with head held low. The knob turns in his hand, door slides open on dry hinges. He doesn't look the stranger in the face as he retreats to the sanctuary that lies in a musty chair's embrace.

"Gray," says the stranger into the drifting detrital air. He says it slow, no rush in the word, he with all the time in the world. "You don't look well."

"I look the same as ever."

The stranger lingers in the door, not moving deeper into the room, content only to hover in silhouette, light of moon or buzzing streetlamp or some phantom radiance at his back and left behind, unable to pass and leaving only this, only him to step forward and into the room. He stands that way, a solemn, silent thing in the dark for minutes as he awaits with stoic patience the reaction he's come for.

Gray shatters the stillness with his hushed voice. Words crack in living imitation of the broken quiet.

"Ask your question. I won't do it for you."

The light touches just enough face to show a grin appear in that silhouette, the shade's face contorting as lips pull hard at edges.

"Would you like to come along, Gray?"

Gray doesn't answer right away. When he finds his voice it is smaller still, someone else's words finding their way from his dry lips.

"How long will this go on?"

"That's really up to you."

"What am I being punished for?"

The stranger considers this for only a moment.

"What makes you think you're being punished at all?"

"I could kill you."

"You could."

Gray wants to respond, thinks he will respond, but there is nothing to say and his hands make fists that are useless, wastes, a vain rage so impotent that even the pounding of those fists into padded chair arms seems far beyond the infinite reach of dream. The stranger cuts the moment with mocking words.

"Would you like to come along?"

The light flickers at the stranger's back, its presence diminished but not gone as Gray stares into the darkness without looking away, not thinking but only wishing for a choice, any choice beyond what there remains for him. When at last he's done he responds in a whisper.

"I want you to leave now."

The stranger only nods, receiving what he's expected and what he always receives. He turns from the room with its haunted silence and the dust of ages. He goes without drama, without word, no waves from cold hand holding hat nor from the one stuffed in the pocket of a coat that only gains substance as the light from rows of lamps lining suburban streets at last reach to stroke its fine fabrics. A nice coat, something made with the attention and care of an artisan, hands skilled in its design. Hand sets hat on head, hiding away the neatly trimmed haircut combed to one side in antiquated severity. Gray looks from the vantage of the doorway to the withdrawing hat and its owner as he's done so many times before, an ancient hat with brim turned up in elegant pomp. This is the last Gray sees as he turns away, no interest in seeing what happens when the stranger goes, whether he turns to smoke and dissipates or merely walks ever into the distance, a prosaic meandering in and out of existence as shadow envelopes the space between lamps.

Blocks away music caresses the night, a rolling hum that moves the ground so slightly, a thing to be both felt and heard and if someone is angry at this nighttime presence their protests are insignificant, easily shrugged off. Dots of humanity appear a street over, two streets over, young bodies moving from a bar to a party or from a party to a bar, soft skin and laughing voices appearing in transitory bliss in the scant space between trees and homes, obstacles that separate these ephemeral apparitions from the place where Gray sees and hears and finally, as the bodies vanish and the music dies and the world goes away, stepping inside, he closes the door.

4.

A hum begins, white noise smoothing away the vestiges of an already waning dream. The hum becomes a grating vibration as somewhere nearby machinery shifts into active gear. Mower. Gray breathes in and rises from sleep. Noise swells and recedes but never ceases. Arms stretch and legs touch floor as he sits up amid the pulsating din. He dresses in no rush as destruction swirls ever inward in the rise and fall of sound. His tie is straight as he sits once more on the bed's unmade edge and waits for the sound to die away. Sometime later, it does.

He opens the door at the second knock. A child stands on the porch looking up.

"I cut your grass."

The boy waits for payment or acknowledgement of the deed and the words. Gray stares back, no imbursement save an unchanged offering of the passage of time.

"I've seen you," says the child.

"What?"

"Some nights you talk to that man."

Gray says nothing.

"How long have you been here."

"A long time."

"What do you do?"

"I'm a salesman."

"No you're not. How do you live?"

The invasive disposition of such a question passes over Gray in waves of revulsion. He waits for the boy to lose interest in his own line of thought, but the boy stands spellbound by the shameless curiosity of innocence.

"Some friends died," says Gray. "They left me some money."

"You're weird."

Gray hands the boy a folded ten-dollar bill and closes the door. The creak of boards mark the boy's exit from the porch. The sound of the mower being dragged across the lawn and down the street follows, and soon the world returns with all its delicate rumblings.

***

The park is a mess of hives, each one a pocket universe. Cliques meander past imagined cordons to view but not approach those foreign inhabitants of the section adjacent; the exiled grandfathers with their games at stone tables, pieces moving with patience and method, the nannies observing the children they're tasked with while each child bounces with delighted ignorance through their own imagined infinity. Couples walk along cracked sidewalk lanes and here and there a straggler from the lunch crowd sits working over the remnants of some deli concoction, but the clusters do not mingle and each is easily defined.

Gray sits on a bench by the old men at their tabletop diversion, but he makes no effort to be among them, and if any among their ranks take notice of him where he sits, none bother to speak up. He used to read in this place, used to sit here for long days with some book or other held open in lap, but now he only sits, the motion of existence telling a story longer and more intricate than any finite narrative. The churning of these fleeting wraiths manifests in patterns felt but impossible to follow, an organized chaos calculable only by an eye existing somewhere on the outside of it all, a being a step back from the unending swirl and flow of life.

Gray takes it in; the face of a woman wrinkling as she chides a child for a playtime transgression, a geriatric man's hard eyes taking the measure of his chessboard opponent, dogs walked at leash end and treats sold from rolling carts and grinning fools pointing at something unseen, a sight existing outside the mechanical rotations of the park habitation, the suggestion of worlds beyond this. Gray is an unmoving cog amidst this impossible machine, only an audience to the tragic wash of story all around, and when hours have gone by and the sun begins to fall away, face placid as wraiths pass along sidewalk, a hello tossed by a woman jogging in garish spandex suit, he stands and walks to the street.

Streetlights hum as he passes beneath. Unblemished sidewalk leads the way past each home indistinguishable from the last. No one takes notice of this tattered phantom moving among their transitory lives in a faded suit, a dented felt hat planted hard on a downturned head that watches unblinking the passage of block after block underfoot. He doesn't see them and he doesn't see the world. Shapes in the fog of his malaise. He doesn't have to look up to know every detail that he passes. He's seen them all a thousand times before.

The sights on Gray's street are the same as those of each that's come before but for the leaning husk of his home. The steps are silent under a tread barely felt. Opens the front door to a rush of stale air. He pauses in the doorway, looks to the side. A policeman draped in the regalia of authority knocks on a neighbor's door, asking questions about a child gone missing. Gray shuts his own door, and with it, the world.

***

The knock comes at night, an expected disturbance. Gray doesn't get up. He could not keep the thing on the other side shut out if he wanted to. The knock comes again. He waits, staring. Dust drifts on air, slow movement caught in light of streetlamps filtering in through windows, the sprinklings of life's detritus coasting along to nowhere in particular. The knock does not come a third time.

The knob turns and the door opens and the stranger removes hat, crosses the threshold as if he's been invited, as if he's wanted in this place. Fetid air plumes as he falls into a chair. Dust motes swirl. Dead eyes look out from the impossibly ordinary face of the stranger. He lounges, one leg resting across the other, hat in lap, content to play a waiting game he knows he'll win with ease.

Gray slumps in his seat as he breaks with a single word steeped in futility.

"Why?"

No humor exists in the slow spread of smile upon the stranger's face.

"Jarring, isn't it. Remembering what anger feels like."

"There was no need."

"He saw me," says the stranger

"He was no one."

"He saw me. He remembered me. That's all it takes."

Gray falls into a grim silence, any words in him only a vain flailing, not worth the attempt. The stranger sits with him in that quiet, contented in the minute he allows that calm to exist before he speaks in a voice pregnant with mocking sympathy.

"The ugliness of this world is nothing new. You can leave with me if you want. We can go right now."

No change passes over Gray, only the in and out of breath and then a single terse thought loosed upon the room.

"Get out."

The stranger carries his hat across the doorsill and out into the night, leaving Gray alone in his slumped misery, slatted light illuminating only pieces of this musty cave world and its one unmoving inhabitant. A hand tightens on the arm of a chair. Teeth grind in mute rage. Some time later the swirl of dust in the air has calmed, and nothing moves in this solemn place for long night hours.

5.

He sips from a glass of tepid water without any real need. Gray's hat sits alongside a hand placed stoic on countertop. Wait staff move about, setting plates before hungry customers, gathering tips, taking orders. Snippets of conversation pass by in the haze. An earnest upset consumes talk. Gray watches foot traffic move by along sidewalk on the street side of long windows lining diner walls, or he watches the room he inhabits, himself apart from the passing swirl of chatter.

She's there, planted at a corner booth, a pen scribbling its way across a page. Scratch paper, a part of something torn away from a whole. A plate of some unrecognizable mush sits congealing, forgotten. She chews on the pen cap as she works over a thought. Eyes staring at paper, at what they find there, some thought she's put down and already left behind. Lips curl upward, amused or pleased. He looks at her when he's not looking at the passing flow outside. She sees him looking, meets his eyes. He looks away but it's too late.

The slap of her paper, of the notepad she's pulled it from, these mark her presence without his turning to see. She orders a coffee and takes the stool next to his. A fat server with a sincere look of disinterest sets her coffee down and vanishes. She sips and goes back to writing, waiting for the introduction he isn't going to offer.

Her coffee goes cold. She orders another.

"You look familiar."

She doesn't know she's going to say it until she already has. He turns at the sound, flinches at the upset to the natural order of things. The flow of traffic along the sidewalk has become interrupted. The world stands still. Her next coffee arrives.

"I look like anybody," says Gray. He sees the promise of as yet unformed conversation spring forth in the expectant look on her face, a pleasing escape into all the things not yet said that soon will be, and from this he lowers his eyes.

"I can't speak to you."

The crisp noise of a newspaper fluttering without reason across the island breaks the moment. Chester returns his eyes to the crossword there, a smirk on his face as he wholly misreads the situation.

"Well," says the woman, a nameless woman sitting to Gray's side, already slipping back into the scratch page filled with a letter to some other life.

Gray puts a dollar under his glass and leaves his seat. He murmurs an apology to no one in particular and abandons himself to the flow of life outside, moving among its kinetic advance without ever being a part of it.

***

Undiscerning shoppers mill around a warehouse of clothing overstock, hands touching items on racks without interest, rubbing fabric and moving on. A woman frowns at a sheer sundress hanging limp from hanger clasps. A man tries on a suit jacket several sizes too large, shoulders slack, arms loose, the man dwarfed inside like a child bedecked in the trappings of an elder. Along the walls door after door leads to inner suites containing boutiques of finer articles and the craftsmen skilled in their design. The hatter fills the doorway of his shop with his gaunt, unmoving form. A gargoyle, passive in place, eyes sunken deep in skull, glints in the dark of their sockets, watching unblinking, cheekbones protruding.

"There was a man here before," says Gray, only now aware that the instrument intended to explain his story is absent, the dented hat forgotten or lost. Empty hands wave in vain frustration. The hatter's response renders any explanation unnecessary.

"I know the man. He hasn't been in."

Gray looks into the dark pits in that skull, measuring what he finds there. The road to any answers sought is not in this place. He nods once and quits of this unswerving, unpleasant man.

***

The sun is still up as he finds himself, Gray does, standing before the painting, his interest taken by the suggestion of a man in that waving field. The room is silent, the noise of the world shut out by the door Gray passed through seconds or hours ago, somewhere in time before now. He's waiting, he suspects, for the arrival of the stranger, and he wonders who it is the man in the painting waits for.

The knock comes too soon. The sun is falling somewhere beyond dusty blinds, but daylight still filters in. He opens the door.

She stands in silence with the hat held out. His shoulders slump. It's too late.

"You might as well come in."

She crosses the threshold and glides with a relaxed gait through the swirling gloom within. Gray holds out a hand toward an empty chair. Sit. He slumps into his own seat, slim bars of light crossing his person as the sun dies outside.

"Your hat," she says. The dented felt passes from her possession to his like a piece falling into place, a bauble from some other era or world slipping back into its own reality. He settles in his seat, resigned to what is coming. She rests, unmoved by the gloom or the person staring unblinking at her presence. She speaks.

"You were rude to me."

He touches the hat with one hand, letting it sit in his lap but not daring to let the touch end.

"It doesn't matter now."

She crosses one leg over the other. Air stirs, dust animated, glitter spinning in swaths of light. She holds out a hand and coughs up a frustrated word.

"Well?"

"Why did you come here?"

"You ran off."

"I'm cursed."

"What?"

"I was rude to you because I can't talk to you. I can't talk to you because I'm cursed."

"Oh," she says. "You're a lunatic."

"Maybe."

"You tell people that a lot?"

"That I'm cursed?"

"Yeah."

"I don't tell anyone that. Ever."

"Why not?"

"Don't be scared."

"That's ominous."

"I'm being punished. I can't die."

"You really are a crazy person."

"I'm being punished with life. People disappear all around me and I am left to suffer forever."

"That sounds like a bad deal."

"It's a curse. It's not supposed to sound nice."

"Like in the bible. The end times. The good people get to go to Heaven while everybody else gets left here."

"Not like that. Not at all like that."

She sits back.

"Sounds a lot like it to me."

He only stares back.

"Who disappears?" she asks.

"The rules aren't written down someplace. I don't know who they'll take. I don't know what will and won't set it off. I can't risk it."

"They?"

"I don't know what to call them. There's the stranger, but he works for someone else."

"You should be on antipsychotics."

"Well," he says, but there is nothing to follow with and he falls into a sullen silence. She breaks it.

"How do you know?"

"How do I know what?"

"You can't die. Have you tried stepping in front of a bus?"

"Have I stepped in front of a bus?"

"Yeah."

"I haven't," he says, his face empty of expression. "I have not stepped in front of a bus."

"What if you do?"

"What if I do?"

"You'd know. Then you'd know."

The rough grate of teeth on teeth as his jaw grinds out an implacable rush of emotion is the only noise for a long beat, until at last he speaks up.

"You should leave."

She looks around as if some answer to this sudden shift can be found in the waning light of the room. Her next thought comes out as a dispassionate stream of words.

"You think I'm going to disappear."

"I'm sorry," he says. He holds the door for her as she leaves.

6.

His mouth is parched. He taps his thumb across each finger as he walks. Hands are dry, skin like paper pulled across bone. Each hand flexes with nerves he leaves unacknowledged. He removes his hat and runs a hand through hair, distracting the fidget for seconds. When the hat is back on his head the hands return to their endless, meaningless task. He pauses on the sidewalk before he gets to the door. People ignore his presence as the morning pedestrian flow ambles on in its own serene disinterest.

The door handle is cool in his hand. He pulls and the seal is broken, a blast of coffee and bread and morning world smells wafting through the opening. Chester taps a pen on the counter, stares into a newspaper. A young woman chats with a customer. A geriatric with cold eyes accepts crumpled dollar bills from a man who only bought coffee. Life swirls in the room. Gray moves among that teeming froth.

There is a rush to things, an urgency felt in the moment that has been absent for long years. Twinges of some ugly emotion from a past life. Hands squeeze into fists. He steps deep into the room until the room's nooks show themselves. She's there, seated and oblivious at her table. Hands loosen, each palm white, drained of life. He exhales a breath he didn't know he was holding. She's smiling, she's chatting. Gray steps forward and through the shuffling breakfast crowd the stranger's ordinary face appears, innocuous and nodding, engaged in talk with the woman at the table. He stops, one foot forward, paused in place as all around the world fails to notice the change.

She doesn't turn. The stranger speaks, his words eaten by the room. She nods, absolute agreement with some unheard lie. Gray watches and waits and it goes on this way, this moment unending. He turns away when he finds he can.

Chester's pen is dying. He taps it against the countertop, shakes it, prints letters carefully in empty crossword spaces, shakes the pen again. Gray is standing at his side for seconds, for a minute, content to wait to be noticed.

"Gray?"

Gray's face is placid, empty. His voice comes out without feeling.

"I need a gun."

The questions that come to Chester's mind circle once, retreat unasked. He looks back at the cold man before him.

"Come back tonight."

Gray gives only a bare nod. Hands are stuffed into pockets as he walks away. Chester watches the exit of this stranger he's sat across from on an untold number of mornings. He watches the door and the sidewalk traffic. Hand taps pen on counter to the beat of some unspoken thought. He looks back at his paper, working to remember where he was. He puts pen to paper, but the pen has run dry. He runs the point over the same spot again and again without leaving its mark. Chester folds the page over, the puzzle unfinished.

***

A stillness creeps among the racks of suits between which Gray moves. The shoppers have gone or not yet arrived. The air is thin, untouched by human lungs. A mechanical sound drones inside a wall, an air conditioner circulating for no one. The hatter's booth stands open, the door open, unguarded. An elderly man sits, one leg over the other, his form lounging prim and polite in one of the room's used-up, spent chairs. The man smiles a wide smile, his wrinkled face a mask of affable delight. One hand touches a derby resting in his lap while the other hand points to an empty chair in courteous invite. Gray closes the door behind him as he enters.

"Are you waiting for the hatter?"

The elderly looks back at Gray, at this wasted question. His response is delayed.

"The hatter is gone."

Gray sits, settling into the chair's worn grooves. The elderly watches him with eternal patience, ancient eyes studying this creature moving before them.

"I came looking for you."

"No answers to find," says the elderly. "No wisdom here."

"You're like me. You're trapped."

The elderly laughs at this, unashamed guffaws in the face of Gray's sincerity.

"We're all trapped. We're stuck. The terms of your agreement don't matter. What you did, I don't care. I can't help you and you can't help you. I'm like you? Okay. I'm like you. Sure. What does that get you? Nothing. Nothing."

The elderly stands. He puts the derby on his head, that dark fabric soaking up the light of the room, swallowing it all.

"There," he says. "Now you're wise."

***

Streetlamps buzz as he passes beneath, in and out of their pooled, pale light. Birds line wires strung from utility poles, oil-black menacing things, wings wet with their own grim color. They sing a manic song that Gray ignores, his attention turned wholly to a futile conviction. Street traffic is limited, cars heard but not seen, foot traffic stifled, disinterested passersby appearing along the way, soon gone again.

The diner is a hot, humid cave. A bulb has burned out in one corner and the room basks in dreamlike illumination, shadows moving through unearthly light. Gray orders a coffee. He drinks it down and orders another. A newspaper sits forgotten on the counter opposite him, its page folded to the crossword. He stares at this paper, at the empty seat at its side.

The booth where the woman sat is empty. The seat from which she laughed at some private joke, where she scribbled letters to a better life, this place is bereft of its former meaning. Now it is only a place, a seat to be taken. He leaves a generous tip on his way out.

The stranger won't be there yet, at the leaning, warped home Gray inhabits, but he will be waiting for the time to come when he is to make an appearance. The stranger is off wherever he goes, but the time is approaching. Gray stands on an empty sidewalk looking out at a darkened sky. Streetlamps buzz. Signs inviting miscreants in out of the darkness mark shops still open into evening hours or later. They hum, glowing with their own internal life, the places and their signs. A wind moves along the sidewalk, a chill that passes through Gray in his place out here, his face unmarked by all the years as even the sidewalk beneath his feet gives up its scars, cracks of age showing the world inside. A bus comes along on an avenue named after some long dead crofter who inhabited this place before there was a street to name or even a city. The engine growls like some arcane beast. Gray steps off the curb. There is no sound of brakes.

HAPPINESS
BECOMES
YOU
VENAFRI PRINCIPEM NOMENTI MARCHIONĒ,
ET CELANI COMITEM MERITISSIMVM
Cum Indice memorabilium, nec non uariarũ linguarũ locupletissimo.
DOMINIVM
Sumptibus M. Antony Bernię Bibliopolę Bononiensis
VIGILANTIA
Coll. S. Andrea Poenit. Bon.
SALVS
IMMORTALITAS
BONONIÆ, apud Clementem Ferronium MDCXXXX Superiorũ permissu
Col. S. Andreæ Poenit. Bon.

He sat in an upstairs bedroom with a blanket draped over withered legs he'd never need again. A bay window looked out on an open field that once grew acres of swaying grain. Voices that once sang and laughed in the rooms below now erupted with shrieks or sobs or broke altogether.

His chair rocked forward as he strained to look at the sky. Bright constellations grown to a billion year adolescence had all but winked out in one disinterested huff. Existence itself seemed to know just when its time had come.

Fires consumed the land that once had been those soft fields. Stars fell from a dying sky in a vain attempt to save themselves. Black swallowed everything but the tiniest red seen through its hazy pelt, and there was no sanity in that red, only the promise of all eternal hell.

He leaned back in his chair and pulled the blanket up high on his ruined legs. He looked out the room's one huge window at the barefoot being that strode through the ashen scape and he allowed himself a last cynical smile.

And soon all was quiet in the house.

Summaries of Stories Included

The Weather Maker follows a man as he blames the local TV meteorologist for the weather and by extension the ills of the world.

Morning Stockton tells the story of a man finding (and stealing) a written history of an imaginary town while at a party and learning how seeking something that doesn't exist can consume.

Drowning is the story of a woman drowning in tears above an empty pool as she mourns the loss of her pool-boy and implied lover.

In *The Rails* a young man visits a rail yard to hear a transient there tell legends from his days of hopping trains that may inspire horror or hope.

A man believes he's witnessed a suicide that likely did not happen. *In Loving Memory of Patricia Flowers*. It's a story of misplaced guilt and its lingering effects.

The Farmer's Solution follows a motorist's encounter with a stranger and their discussion of obligation to the past.

A man is bumped into by a stranger. When asked why he doesn't do something about it the man's answer brings consequences. *A Man with Goals*.

Modern Romance tells the story of a woman who makes a connection with a man she's crank called.

The Lock and the Door is the story of a man finding a door in his new home that has no opposite on the wall's reverse. His quest to find the key that gets it open takes him to an attic full of ancient letters, a tomb beneath the town courthouse, and the heir to an architect living in an elder care facility.

Man in Leaf. This story draws parallels between looking at a painting and being in one.

Doing Time is a story about guilt and hats.

Happiness Becomes You acts as a discussion of a world existing on the other side of a window. Also it should be a postcard. Close your eyes. See it? Tell me I'm wrong.

***

Drift. The story follows a bible salesman as he drifts further from the job, continuing to take book orders while cashing the checks himself.

AN EXCERPT FROM CRAIG RODGERS' UPCOMING NOVEL DRIFT

1.

There is a roar from underneath, an unending rush of some great force that will not be ignored. These old roads are just that way, hard-packed blacktop shrieking at the passage of beasts above, a road noise so loud that the tinny bars of some saccharine pop classic playing out of cheap door speakers is almost lost completely.

His name is Charlie, a tag which is stamped in affirmative bold on the card he's supposed to hand with a dimple-filled smile to each new client. A stack of these cards rattles around the glove box, a rubber band holding them together as its elastic slowly dries and its purpose slips away. Sales, says the card with a lackadaisical flair for its own ambiguity. A bible sits on the dash vibrating to the beat of the pavement's roar. The cover is made up of the same intense blue as the sky.

In the distance hangs the hazy suggestion of a city, a prefab dream full of right angles existing on the horizon. Between this place and that is a vast emptiness cleaved by a single line whose unfolding is more or less straight while to each side washes a tide of yellow grassland and here and there the awkward bends of a sleeping tree. No one passes in the opposing lane. Any traveler found in these miles of desolation has but one destination before them.

His tie is loose but still tied, the slack bulge of knot still intact. He paid a motel maid five dollars to tie it for him. The knot always looks wrong when he does it himself.

2.

A slack face is what he wears until the very moment the door opens before him, letting free the heady aroma of perfume and life to waft with lazy abandon into the scentless second floor hallway of a modern, dull complex of office suites. A smile appears with professional timing as he turns his face upon the prosaic figure of a young woman standing in the doorway. Her disinterest sways and falls away as she finds Charlie in her way. She stops short, one foot raised and dropped before the step it was about to take.

"I knocked," he says without real commitment. Maybe he did knock, maybe it's true.

She looks down the hallway, first one way and then the other. A man several doors down stands paused outside another suite, his attention utterly engrossed in the banal particulars of some paperwork in hand.

Charlie is already talking as he slips past the woman.

"I brought along a few samples. Same stuff we have on the website, but, come on. You can't really get a sense of what you're buying that way. A person wants to smell the ink. They want to feel what they're getting."

She shuts the door and follows him through another doorway. Inner office. He remains standing, lounging against a desk with one hand and letting the sample case dangle from the other as the woman rounds the stained oak frame, putting the bulk of the workstation between Charlie and herself.

"You're early."

She says it with a casual bite, not quite accusatory and not quite not.

"I'm punctual," he counters, all dimples and ease.

They talk, him going on about books, her talking price versus volume. She brings up the website, he cranes so he can see. She pivots the monitor, he comes around the desk. He points out items with a pinky, drawing attention to what he wants her to want. He uses words like leather and guarantee. He tells her to enter his name in the box on the right when she places her order. A discount, he says.

His hand moves slow as he retrieves the sky blue book from the sample case. He lets her touch it, lets her run a hand over the contoured surface, half a smile pulling at the corner of her mouth.

He has her.

She handles the business for three churches in town. The order she makes covers all three. He leaves her with a demure tome the color of mud. Her eyes are on the book she holds as he slips the blue sample back into the case. She isn't looking as he nods and smiles and is already gone.

The smile is erased as the door closes at his back. He looks out of a slack face, giving away nothing. The man at the end of the hall looks up from the paperwork in his hand. He nods in vague human connection. Charlie walks in the other direction.

***

He doesn't know the name of the town. This morning he knew, or this morning he'd read it, let his eyes linger long enough to commit it to the scant strip of memory he knew himself willing to part with as the day progressed, and there, now, the name of the town is gone, another place he's already left behind even if the rest of him is still hours from that fated parting.

Gravel crunches under worn tires as he wheels into the motel lot. He parks alongside a beast of a car. Long black hardtop, whitewalls unsullied. 50s, maybe. An ancient thing. The company car from which Charlie emerges is a blight, a dull thing with every edge rounded and bland and utterly without heart. He pauses on loose ground, a hunger swelling, part of him taken by the thought of crossing the street to a chain eatery full of unbound ties and toothy carnivores while some other part of him wishes he'd already gotten a room, was now asleep, was not here at this moment having to make this decision. Somewhere nearby windows shake in their frames under the rumbling passage of an unseen train.

He takes the sample case along as tired feet drag him across the street, not looking this way or that for the aggressive surge of looming traffic, but no traffic comes to prevent this passing.

Sound rises with the door's opening. A muted yellow world inside, the glow of dim lights and the hovering scent of meat and grease crowd the senses, a palpable presence that coats. A hostess presents a manic grin and wide, haunting eyes that Charlie looks too long into, unable to turn from the unrelenting draw they offer without shame.

"Just one?"

She says it without malice but he flinches just the same.

"Smoking," and as an afterthought, "please."

The grin persists and those haunting eyes do not blink.

"We no longer have a smoking section in the dining area but you're welcome to smoke on the patio."

A man with sleeves rolled to elbows cuts at a burned slab of meat at the single table outside. On his head is a bowler hat, its cloth dented, lived in. Charlie doesn't look at a menu, mumbles the first thing that comes to mind.

"Reuben sandwich."

Her grin does not change.

"I'm the hostess."

He stares blankly back.

"I'm not your waitress."

If there is more he does not hear. The bag in his hand is an albatross that pulls at his arm as he makes his slow way, weaving between tables and the lives of strangers existing and seething in loud jubilation in the path of every away. Writhing mass of life. Utensils scrape across glassware and mouths cackle. As Charlie breaks through the other side the door is there, the world just on the other side. A waitress passes, smiles a sane smile. She does not belong here. He orders his sandwich, points to the table outside, more words caught somewhere between himself and his mouth but she understands and nods and is soon gone to make things happen. He takes a seat at the patio table.

The man with the steak puts out a gloved hand, his palm turned up in vague acquiescence, an acceptance that this is happening. Sit, it says, but Charlie already has. The gloves have no fingers, their cloth cut away and the remains frayed. A dusty relic, this man. The lump of a cigarette pack stands out in the pocket of a waistcoat. Shrewd eyes of a carnival barker, some dustbowl urchin now wandered in out of the past. The man goes back to cutting, the knife going through line after line of the meat.

"Put you at the kids table, too," says the man. He takes no bites between cuts, taking care to slice each piece and move it aside as he goes to the next, preparing but not eating. "There's no ashtray."

A lit cigarette sits balanced on the lip of an empty coffee cup. The lightest touch from wind would upset its delicate state, but the day is still, paused in waiting.

"You a local?"

"I don't want to buy anything. I don't want anything."

The man laughs. "Just conversation. Just making conversation," he says.

Charlie shakes his head. The man finishes his cuts and places the knife on a napkin.

"Me neither. What do you do?"

"Sales. Traveling sales. I facilitate purchases while acting as the national face of the company."

The man takes a fork in hand but doesn't eat.

"That sounds like a prepared statement."

“It is,” says Charlie. “I go around reminding people that every few years they need to replace books handled by grubby hands on a regular basis. Sounds better the other way.”

The man takes a bite of the charred meat. His face is neutral, placid. Teeth grind in silence. He swallows and speaks.

“Is it a good job?”

“It’s an easy job. I meet the appointments someone else makes and I help people buy what they already want. I drive a lot. I drive all the time.”

The man goes on eating, forking small bites of meat and chewing, one after another without comment for minutes. If he feels an awkwardness in the quiet he leaves before him it does not show. The restaurant’s side door opens and lets loose the banging cacophony of its inner horror. The confused patron in the doorway looks around, brow curling over brooding eyes. The madness at its back pulls that formless ape back inside and slams the door in its wake.

The man stops eating halfway through the steak. He sets the fork next to the knife. Napkin soaks grease. The weak blue of the table can be seen underneath. He’s slow to look up, speaking before he does.

“Is that satisfying work?”

“No.”

A waitress appears, a different face from the last, this one a stranger. She brings Charlie’s sandwich and if she speaks it is a perfunctory friendliness. The man in the bowler smokes in silence and Charlie eats and soon it is clear there is nothing more to say. The man nods and only that as he stands and turns and walks on thick-soled boots around a corner and away. It is only now that Charlie realizes the man said nothing about himself.

A pack of cigarettes sits nestled in a pocket of the suit coat that hangs limp on Charlie's sunken frame. He thinks about smoking but doesn't. He puts a ten-dollar bill under the cup of ashes, then puts down another two singles. He doesn't wait for the check. The long black classic is gone when he crosses back to the motel. The lot is half empty, slots filled at random and no two alike. A bag with essentials is forgotten, toiletries and clothes and the all-purpose baubles of everyday life left behind in the company car as he passes. His one clasped bag, the sample case, comes along to the motel check-in.

He pays for the room with a company card without saying two words to the clerk at the front desk. The clerk doesn't notice. A television plays a talk show in a foreign language, the sets decked out in vibrant 70s chic. A host shows teeth and nods a lot. He moves his hands when he talks. The topic is impossible to guess. A current events piece about a clown. Charlie takes the room key.

The motel room smells like someone's dinner, a nameless spice floating on the air in a lusty heat. Cooking in the next room, or not. Maybe a room further down, somewhere distant, a place only connected through the labyrinthine meanderings of a duct system. Charlie doesn't care. He drops the sample case on the floor and falls to the bed. He's already asleep when his phone begins to ring.

Craig Rodgers has published a few books and intends to publish a few more before he fakes his own death.

www.ingramcontent.com/pod-product-compliance
Lightning Source LLC
Chambersburg PA
CBHW021703110726
47902CB00007B/2040

9781088024645